Words, pictures & design
Recipes kindly supplied by bartenders named in each recipe & edited by Simon Difford
Other words by Simon Difford & Sammy Hemmings
Cocktail photography by Dan Malpass
Design by Dan Malpass
Printed in UK by The Westdale Press Ltd
Produced for Caorunn Gin by Odd Firm of Sin Limited
Published by Inver House Distillers Ltd

Caorunn Cocktail Collection

Introduction

CAORUNN COCKTAIL COLLECTION

Every day, around the world, thousands of gin cocktails are enjoyed. From enduring classics to modern innovations, the range of mixing possibilities is vast, and exciting. What a shame then that bartenders' creations all too often stay within the confines of their bar. How many of these cocktails are forgotten, never to be recreated or enjoyed again after they are taken off the menu to make way for the next? This book aims to change that.

Caorunn, the premium hand-crafted Scottish gin, selected and then invited 500 of the world's best bartenders to be a part of an exciting initiative to find, promote and share their best gin cocktails. From the hundreds of cocktails these bartenders submitted the following were selected to feature in this book, the Caorunn Cocktail Collection, handily grouped into long and short drinks.

Many of the cocktails featured in this book were inspired by Caorunn's five Celtic foraged botanicals: Rowan Berries, Heather, Coul Blush Apples, Dandelion and Bog Myrtle, all handpicked by Gin Master, Simon Buley from the hills surrounding the breath-taking setting of Balmenach Distillery in the Cairngorms National Park. "There is no better feeling than savouring drinks made with hand-picked ingredients. Not only do they taste better, but it also connects you to the natural world and the wonders on offer," says Buley.

One of those foraged botanicals, Coul Blush red apples, also inspired this gin's signature G&T made with well-chilled fizzing tonic and slices of red apple to highlight this gin's aromatic flavour profile, described as "a modern London Dry Gin with a dry and crisp, aromatic taste adventure and a long dry finish."

Simon personally makes each small 1,000 litre batch of Caorunn Gin and talking to him it quickly becomes apparent that making

Caorunn, which he created, is a labour of love. While he works at the Balmenach Distillery, in the remote and beautiful Scottish Highlands, the gin he makes is enjoyed, appreciated and mixed by bartenders around the world. One craftsman making a gin to in turn be crafted into a delicious cocktail by others. This book serves as a fitting tribute to the craft of one distiller and many bartenders. Enjoy.

Difford's Guide Caorunn Gin tasting notes.

Apperance
Crystal clear.

Bouquet
Citrusy and floral with pine-fresh juniper and black pepper spice. It may be the power of suggestion, but there's also faint ripe red apple.

Taste
Fresh, superbly clean and balanced with piney juniper, zesty citrus, mild black pepper spice, light fruitiness and faint floral notes. Almost creamy, rounded mouthfeel.

Aftertaste
Long, cleansing, lightly spiced piney juniper finish which fades with cracked black pepper spice. Very faint chocolate powder note.

Overall
Pronounced piney juniper - as you'd expect from a proper gin, with floral complexity and a rounded mouthfeel.

Cheers
Simon Difford

The Distillery

BALMENACH DISTILLERY, MORAY, SCOTLAND

VAT Nº 3
CAP 4,225 LITRES

FEINT
TANK 1

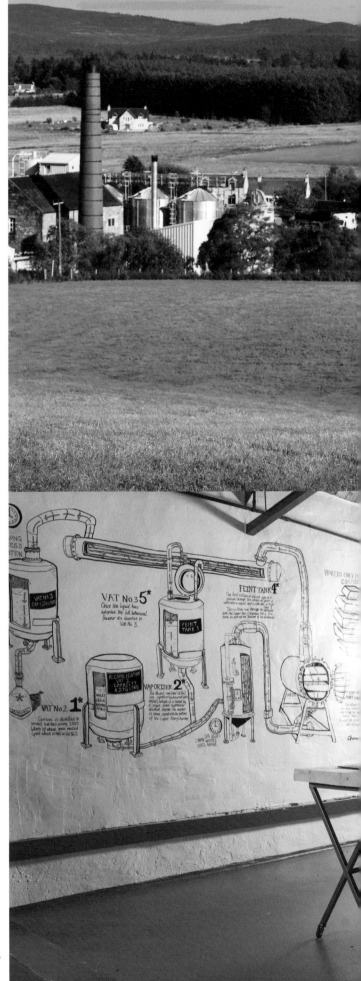

CAORUNN GIN

Caorunn, pronounced 'ka-roon', is the Gaelic word for rowan berry which, along with dandelion, bog myrtle, heather and Coul Blush apple, comprise the five Celtic botanicals out of 11 total botanicals used to flavour this proudly Scottish gin.

As well as drawing on Celtic heritage, Caorunn takes advantage of something else uniquely Scottish: the country's reputation for whisky distilling. Caorunn draws upon these skills and is, in fact, made by a whisky distiller, Simon Buley at the Balmenach (single malt whisky) distillery in the Scottish Highlands.

THE BALMENACH DISTILLERY

The Balmenach distillery lies in the Speyside whisky region within the Cairngorms National Park at the foot of the Haughs of Cromdale. The distillery is situated on a road which runs through the nearby village of Cromdale towards one of the oldest crossing points of the River Spey. Ruins of an old castle stand on the hill of Tom Lethendry behind the distillery, where in 1690 Jacobite soldiers took refuge after the battle of the Haughs of Cromdale.

In the early 1800s, three brothers, the McGregors from Tomintoul, set up a farm on the land with one of the brothers, James, operating an illicit still. In 1823 the Excise Act, which sanctioned the distilling of whisky in return for a licence fee and payment of duty per gallon, was enacted. The following year, in 1824, James obtained one of the new licences, so formally establishing his distillery under the name Balminoch, making it one of the oldest distilleries in the Speyside region.

The present-day Balmenach name was introduced in 1897 when the distillery was incorporated as the Balmenach Glenlivet Distillery Company. The distillery remained in the hands of the McGregor family until 1922 when it was acquired by a consortium which in turn went onto become part of Distillers Company Limited (DCL), which we know today as Diageo.

Balmenach was mothballed in 1993 and lay silent until 1998 when its present owners, Inver House Distillers, acquired the distillery and resumed Scotch whisky production in March of the same year.

CAORUNN'S BOTANICAL RECIPE

When Inver House Distillers decided to start making gin, Simon Buley, one of the malt whisky distillers at the Balmenach Distillery, and something of a gin aficionado, was tasked with creating the new gin. He lives near the distillery and it was to the hills of the National Park in which the distillery sits that he looked for both inspiration and ingredients.

Consequently, while Caorunn's recipe includes six traditional gin botanicals: juniper, coriander, lemon peel, orange peel, angelica root and cassia bark, its character comes from five Celtic botanicals, all of which grow profusely in the countryside surrounding the distillery. These are rowan berries, Coul Blush apple, heather, bog myrtle and dandelion.

Rowan berries – these are sharp-tasting piquant red berries and in Celtic mythology the rowan is known as the Traveller's Tree because it was believed to prevent travellers from losing their way. Rowan wood's density made it popular for walking sticks and its branches were often used as dowsing rods. As well as being crucial to Caorunn Gin's flavour it also inspired its name. In Gaelic the word for rowan berry is Rudha-an (literally meaning 'red one' and pronounced similarly to English rowan) or more usually, Caorunn (pronounced 'ka-roon').

Heather – covers the Scottish Highlands and lends subtle perfumed undertones with a nuance of honey to Caorunn.

Bog Myrtle – is a deciduous shrub which commonly grows in the peat bogs of the Highlands and gives Caorunn soft, sweet resinous aromas.

Dandelions – have long been used as a herb and impart just a hint of sharpness to Caorunn.

Coul Blush Apple – Britain's most northerly apple first fruited in Coul, Ross-shire in 1827. It has golden coloured skin and sweet, soft, cream flesh.

CAORUNN GIN PRODUCTION

Caorunn Gin is made in the former cask-filling store which sits alongside the still room of the Balmenach malt whisky distillery. The old oak spirit receiver – the huge wooden vat which used to hold the spirit which flowed from the stills before filling the casks – still dominates the space.

Caorunn is made slightly differently from other London-style gins – it's Scottish, after all – but still qualifies as a London Gin. A vapour infusion method is used instead of steeping, but while some other gins are also made by vapour infusion, no other uses a 'Copper Berry Chamber'. This piece of equipment was made in the 1920s, and was originally used for the manufacture of perfumes. The chamber is round and contains four large trays on which the botanicals are spread. As the alcohol vapour slowly rises up through the perforated copper trays it picks up the flavours of the botanicals.

The berry chamber is made from thick copper with external stainless steel encasing insulation. The internal diameter of the chamber is 91cm with a copper frame that holds the four drawer-like perforated horizontal stainless steel trays which present a large surface area of both botanicals and copper. (A much larger surface area than is presented in either the small chambers modern stills incorporate into their lyne arm for vapour infusion, or even the basket at the top of a Carterhead still.) The copper construction of the chamber and trays helps remove sulphates from the spirit and some say softens the gin.

Simon accurately weighs each of the 11 botanicals using a set of Avery scales and carefully spreads some of each botanical evenly over each of the four trays. Although he is understandably cagey about the proportions of each botanical used, he did tell us that each batch uses just under 20kg of botanicals.

Caorunn is distilled in small batches, each using 1,000 litres of wheat grain neutral spirit which is held in Vat No. 2. (The old vats and distilling equipment used have been re-commissioned for use in Caorunn Gin production so consequently are named according to their original plate numbers, rather than the order in which they are used.)

The alcohol runs from Vat No. 2 into Vaporiser No. 2 (nicknamed 'Little Rocket') where it is heated by a steam jacket to produce an alcohol vapour which is piped into the bottom of the berry chamber. Two diffusers ensure the vapours are evenly distributed and directed to rise up through the copper trays spread with botanicals. The now botanical infused vapour leaves the top of the chamber and is piped into the condenser where it cools and returns the alcohol to liquid. This is collected in Vat No. 1. Once the liquid has picked up the flavours and taste of the botanicals the liquid (now Caorunn) is diverted to Vat No. 3.

This process continues until Vat No. 2, the first vat which holds the base neutral spirit, is empty. At this point Simon opens and closes valves to direct first runnings of weakly flavoured spirit from Vat No. 1 into Vaporiser No. 2 and then back up through the botanicals as vapour a second time. Now with more concentrated botanical flavours, the vapour passes through the condenser and this time into Vat No. 3 as concentrated Caorunn Gin.

The whole process takes around seven hours and the initial 1,000 litres of neural spirit yields around 945 litres of gin spirit which is reduced with purified Scottish water to a bottling strength of 41.8% alcohol by volume.

The Drinks

HOW TO MAKE A COCKTAIL

METHODS

By definition, any drink that is described as a cocktail contains more than one ingredient. So if you are going to make cocktails, you have to know how to combine these various liquids.

As in cooking, there is a correct order in which to do things. With a few exceptions, it runs as follows:

1. Select glass and chill or pre-heat (if required)
2. Prepare garnish (if required)
3. Pour ingredients into mixing receptacle
4. Add ice (if required)
5. Mix ingredients (shake, stir, blend, etc.)
6. Strain (or pour) into glass
7. Add pre-prepared garnish (if required)
8. Serve to guest or enjoy yourself

Unlike cooking, where there are a myriad of preparation and cooking methods to master, there are essentially only eight different ways to "mix" a cocktail:

1. Build
2. Shake
3. Stir
4. Blend
5. Throw
6. Roll
7. Swizzle
8. Layer

The last, "layering", isn't strictly mixing. On the contrary, the idea here is to float each ingredient on its predecessor without the ingredients merging at all – think B52 cocktail.

At the heart of every cocktail lies at least one of these eight methods, so understanding these terms is fundamental.

BUILDING

It is common for bartenders and bartending books to say "build in glass". This simply means to combine ingredients in the glass it is to be served in. This is the usual method for making Highball drinks such as a gin & tonic or a whisky & soda.

SHAKERS AND SHAKING

When you see the phrase "shake with ice and strain", or similar, in a recipe, you should place all the necessary ingredients with cubed ice in a cocktail shaker and shake briskly. Don't be shy about it – imagine how you might agitate the metal ball in a can of spray-paint. Shake for around 15 seconds, then strain the liquid into the glass, leaving the ice behind in the shaker.

Shaking not only mixes a drink, it also chills, dilutes and aerates it. The dilution achieved by shaking is just as important to the resulting cocktail as using the right proportions of the ingredients. If you use too little ice it will melt too quickly in the shaker, producing an over-diluted drink – so fill your shaker at least two-thirds full with fresh ice.

Losing your grip while shaking is likely to make a mess and a flying shaker could injure a bystander, so always hold the shaker firmly with two hands and never shake fizzy ingredients (unless in a minute proportion to the rest of the drink).

DRY SHAKE

When making drinks containing cream and eggs it is common practice among some bartenders to first shake the mixture in a shaker without ice, before shaking the drink a second time with ice. (An increasingly common alternative is to shake with ice first and then again without ice.) This practice is known as "dry shaking". The theory is that shaking without ice, and so at a higher temperature, allows the drink to emulsify better.

STIRRERS & STIRRING

Stirring is one of the most basic ways of mixing a cocktail. You might not give much thought to the technique used to stir a cup of tea or even a pot of paint, but somehow cocktails deserve a little more reverence.

Stirring glasses come in a multitude of shapes and sizes. If a specially designed lipped mixing glass is not available, a Boston glass (the glass half of a Boston shaker) or even the base of a standard shaker will suffice.

There are almost as many different styles of bar spoons on the market as there are stirring glasses. Some have spiralling stems, some have flat ends and others have three-pronged fork ends. The key thing is for your spoon to have a long stem so it will

reach down to the base of the glass while allowing you to comfortably hold the stem of the spoon high above the mixing glass.

If a cocktail recipe calls for you to "stir with ice and strain", then you should do so.

• Measure your ingredients into your chilled stirring glass and then two-thirds fill it with ice.

• Hold the bar spoon between your thumb and the first two fingers of your dominant hand, with the spoon's shaft running between your middle finger and ring finger.

• Slide the bowl of the spoon down the inside edge of the glass until it almost touches the base of the glass.

• Keeping your arm still, and to an extent your wrist as well, use your fingers to pull the spoon towards and then away from you, aiming to hit the quarter-hour marks on an imaginary clock-face inside your stirring glass. As the spoon runs around, so it will spin the ice and liquid in the glass, while spinning on its own axis in your fingers.

• Stir briskly for about 30–45 seconds – this should account for at least 50 revolutions.

• Place your strainer into or over the stirring glass (see "straining") and strain into your chilled serving glass. If the recipe calls for the drink to be served over ice, then you should ice your glass first. Never use the ice from the stirring glass in the drink itself.

• The ice used during stirring is now spent and should be dumped, or alternatively can be left in the stirring glass to keep it chilled ready for the next drink. If you do the latter, remember to dump the ice and rinse the glass with cold water before making the next drink.

STRAINING

When straining a shaken drink, a Hawthorn strainer tends to be used, but when straining a stirred drink it is traditional to use a Julep strainer. Both designs of strainer allow the liquid to be poured from the shaker/stirring glass while restraining the spent ice.

Hawthorn strainers have a spring which runs around their circumference to help catch particles of ice and fruit created by the violent act of shaking. They also often have lugs that rest on the rim of the shaker to hold the strainer in position when being used. Most designs of Hawthorn strainer incorporate a ridge or finger rest, which when pushed serves to secure the spring-loaded gap between the strainer and the side of the shaker, allowing finer particles to be caught.

Julep strainers are best described as perforated metal spoons that fit inside the stirring glass. It is said that they take their name from Kentucky gentlemen who would historically hold them over a Mint Julep to keep the ice and mint off their moustaches. Julep strainers are not as efficient at catching small fragments of ice as Hawthorn strainers but are more pleasing to use in conjunction with a stirring glass.

FINE STRAINING

Most cocktails that are served "straight up" – without ice – benefit from an additional strain, over and above the standard Hawthorn strain. This "fine strain" (sometimes also called a "double strain") removes even the smallest fragments of fruit and fine flecks of ice that could float to the surface and spoil the appearance of a drink. Fine straining is not usually necessary when a drink has been stirred, thrown or rolled.

Fine straining is achieved by simply holding a fine sieve, like a tea strainer, between the shaker and the glass.

BLENDING

When a cocktail recipe calls for you to "blend with ice", place all ingredients and ice into a blender and blend to a smooth, even consistency. Ideally, you should use crushed ice as this lessens wear on the blender. Place liquid ingredients in the blender first, adding the ice last. If you have a variable-speed blender, always start slowly and build up speed.

THROWING

Throwing offers more dilution and aeration than simply stirring, but is gentler than shaking. It is achieved by pouring the ingredients from one container to another from a height so the cascading liquid pulls air into the drink.

To do this, assemble your ingredients in the base of your shaker. Add ice and strain into a second large diameter mixing glass/tin with a lipped rim, increasing the distance between the two vessels as you pour – always watch the receptacle you're pouring into, not the one you're pouring from. Now pour the partially mixed cocktail back into the first ice-filled container and strain into the second once again. Repeat this process several times and you will have "thrown" your drink.

ROLLING

Essentially this is a gentle way of mixing using a cocktail shaker. Fill your shaker in the usual manner and then, instead of shaking, gently roll it end-over-end a few times in a tumbling motion. The best-known example of a drink that benefits from being rolled rather than shaken is a Bloody Mary. Rolling maintains the thick mouth feel of the tomato juice, whereas shaking tends to produce a Bloody Mary with a thin texture.

SWIZZLING

To swizzle a drink is simply to stir it using a swizzle stick in a spinning motion. This style of drink mixing originated in the Caribbean, where originally a twig with a few forked branches was used. Today swizzle sticks are usually made of metal or plastic and have several blades or fingers at right angles to the shaft, although some bartending suppliers still sell Caribbean wooden swizzle sticks.

To swizzle, simply immerse the blades of your swizzle stick into the drink. (Swizzled drinks are served with crushed ice.) Hold the shaft between the palms of both hands and rotate the stick rapidly by sliding your hands back and forth against it. If you do not have a bona fide swizzle stick, use a bar spoon in the same manner.

LAYERING

As the name suggests, layered drinks include layers of different ingredients, often in contrasting colours. This effect is achieved by carefully pouring each ingredient into the glass so that it floats on its predecessor.

The success of the technique is dependent on the density (specific gravity) of the liquids used. As a rule of thumb, the less alcohol and the more sugar an ingredient contains, the heavier it is, so the heaviest ingredients should be poured first and the lightest last. Syrups are non-alcoholic and contain a lot of sugar, so they are usually the heaviest ingredient. Liqueurs, which are higher in sugar and lower in alcohol than spirits, are generally the next heaviest ingredient. The exception is cream and cream liqueurs, which can float.

Layering can be achieved by holding the bowl end of a bar spoon (or a soup spoon) in contact with the side of the glass and over the surface of the drink, and pouring slowly over it. The term "float" refers to layering the final ingredient of a cocktail on to its surface.

MUDDLING

Muddling means pummelling fruits, herbs and/or spices with a muddler (a blunt tool similar to a pestle) to gently crush them and release their flavour. You can also use a rolling pin. Just as you would use a pestle and mortar, push down on the muddler with a twisting action.

Only attempt to muddle in the base of a shaker or a suitably sturdy glass. Never attempt to muddle hard, unripe fruits in a glass as the pressure required could break the glass.

MEASURING

The relative proportion of each ingredient within a cocktail is key to making a great drink. Therefore the accuracy with which ingredients are measured is critical to the finished cocktail.

In this book, we've expressed the measures of each ingredient in "shots". Ideally, a shot is 30 millilitres (1 fluid ounce). Whatever your chosen measuring device, it should have straight sides to enable you to accurately judge fractions of a shot.

ICE

A plentiful supply of fresh ice is essential to making good cocktails. If buying bagged ice, avoid the hollow, tubular kind and thin wafers. Instead, look for large, solid cubes.

When filling ice cube trays, use bottled or filtered water to avoid the taste of chlorine that is often apparent in municipal water supplies. Your ice should be dry, almost sticky to the touch. Avoid "wet" ice that has started to thaw.

Whenever serving a drink over ice, always fill the glass with ice, rather than just adding a few cubes. Not only does this make the drink much colder, but the ice lasts longer and so does not dilute the drink.

Never use the same ice in a cocktail shaker twice, even if it's to mix the same drink as before. You should always discard ice after straining the drink and use fresh ice to fill the glass if so required. Pouring the shaken ice into the glass along with the liquid will result in an overly diluted drink that will not be as cold as one where the drink is strained over fresh ice.

CRUSHED ICE

Unless otherwise stated, all references to ice in this book mean cubed ice. If crushed ice is required for a particular recipe, the recipe will state "crushed ice". This is available commercially. Alternatively, you can crush cubed ice in an ice-crusher or simply bash it with a rolling pin in a Lewis bag (a thick canvas bag) or wrapped in a tea towel.

INFUSION AND MACERATION

Infusion simply involves immersing whole herbs, spices, nuts or fruit in alcohol and leaving them to soak until the desired flavours have leached out to flavour the alcohol. When macerating, the botanicals being infused are first broken up/sliced/diced to expose a larger surface area, so allowing the alcohol to leach flavour from more of the botanicals' cells.

Motion, heat and pressure can be applied to increase the rate of extraction. Motion can be as simple as shaking a bottle in which something is being infused every few hours. (In commercial applications infusion often takes place in revolving tanks.) Heating (leaving in a warm place) helps break open the botanical's cells, so allowing the alcohol to more easily extract flavour. Pressure forces the alcohol into the botanical being infused.

Beware of the speed and degree of extraction. A common mistake is to allow over-extraction by adding too much of the flavouring substance or leaving it in the alcohol for too long.

Tea, for example, infuses very quickly and starts releasing unwanted bitter tannins after just five minutes, while vanilla pods can be left for days and hard substances such as nuts for weeks.

GLASSWARE

Cocktails are something of a luxury – you don't just ping a cap and pour. These drinks take a degree of time and care to mix, so they deserve a decent glass.

Before you start, check that your glassware is clean and free from chips and marks such as lipstick. Always handle glasses by the base or the stem to avoid leaving finger marks, and never put your fingers inside a glass.

CHILLING GLASSES

Ideally, glassware should be chilled in a freezer prior to use. This is particularly important for coupette, martini and flute glasses, in which drinks are usually served without ice. It takes about half an hour to sufficiently chill a glass in the freezer. If time is short, you can chill a glass by filling it with ice (ideally crushed, not cubed) and topping it up with water. Leave the glass to cool while you prepare the drink, then discard the ice and water when you are ready to pour. Although this method is quicker than chilling in the freezer, it is not nearly as effective.

PRE-HEATING GLASSES

To warm a glass for a hot cocktail, place a bar spoon in the glass and fill it with hot water, then discard the water and pour in the drink. Only then should you remove the spoon, which is there to help disperse the shock of the heat.

The Drinks

ON-THE-ROCKS & LONG DRINKS

ADAM'S APPLE

Glass: Highball
Garnish: Lemon zest twist (discard)
Method: SHAKE all ingredients with ice and strain into ice-filled glass.

45ml / 1½oz Caorunn Gin
10ml / ⅓oz Crème de cassis
20ml / ⅔oz Freshly squeezed lemon Juice
10ml / ⅓oz Homemade stout reduction
20ml / ⅔oz Cawston Press Apple & Ginger

Origin: Created by Adam Day at Peggy's Bar, Salford, Greater Manchester, England.
Inspiration: Adam says, he was "inspired by the flavours of the Highlands… From the crisp Coul Blush apple to the tart blackcurrant and even its famous malt." By exploring the botanicals of Balmenach, Adam intended to enhance the flavours in Caorunn Gin with locally foraged ingredients. Adam's invigorating concoction comes together for a real Scottish celebration.

APPLE & CAORUNN

Glass: Old-fashioned
Garnish: Orange zest twist & dehydrated apple slice
Method: Blend all ingredients with crushed ice.

45ml / 1½oz Caorunn Gin
(infused with cinnamon)
60ml / 2oz Apple juice
60ml / 2oz Orange juice
20ml / ⅔oz Cointreau liqueur
10ml / ⅓oz Homemade gosella
(gooseberry) syrup

Origin: Created by Jose Antonio Benitez Delgado at Trigueros, Huelva (we've taken the liberty of slightly upping the gin and reducing the apple and orange juice volumes in Jose's recipe).
Inspiration: The infusion of cinnamon gives a light spice. The fruity notes of Jose's cocktail are potent and refreshing, with hints of apple, orange and gooseberry.

BEAUTY & THE BEAST

Glass: Old-fashioned
Garnish: Rosemary sprig, ginger slice & spray red wine
Method: SHAKE all ingredients with ice and strain back into shaker. DRY SHAKE (without ice) and fine strain into chilled glass.

45ml / 1½oz Caorunn Gin
30ml / 1oz Apple juice
30ml / 1oz Freshly squeezed lime juice
15ml / ½oz Homemade rosemary &
ginger syrup
30ml / 1oz Egg white

Origin: Created by Kiettisak Saleephan at Club No. 43, Phuket, Thailand.
Inspiration: The Beauty and the Beast is an enchanting cocktail. With a thick, smooth texture, it looks spectacular, especially its foam top and exquisite garnishes.

BEE SIMPLE

Glass: Sling
Garnish: Mint sprigs & bee pollen
Method: POUR all ingredients into glass filled with crushed ice and churn.

50ml / 1 ⅔oz Caorunn Gin
10ml / ⅓oz Heather honey
3 dashes Orange bitters
25ml / ⅚oz Sparkling water
2 drops Orange blossom water

Origin: Created by Alex Palumbo at White Horse Oyster & Seafood Bar, Edinburgh, Scotland.
Inspiration: "The drink is inspired by the Scottish bees that are the ultimate form of forager in my mind," Alex says, "flying miles to find the perfect flower and pollen." Like Caorunn Gin, which has 5 wild, foraged Scottish botanicals, and 11 botanicals in total. Alex's creation is "a variation of a Julep but with simple and elegant flavours of heather honey, mint, and most of all, gin."

BEE'S FIZZ

Glass: Wine glass
Garnish: Lemon zest twist
Method: SHAKE first 4 ingredients with ice and strain back into shaker. DRY SHAKE (without ice) and strain into chilled glass (no ice). TOP with tonic water.

50ml / 1 ⅔oz Caorunn Gin
20ml / ⅔oz Homemade sour mix
10ml / ⅓oz Wild honey
2 dashes Orange bitters
50ml / 1 ⅔oz Tonic water

Origin: Created by Joel John Timis at Nizza Restaurant at Sofitel, Bukit Damansara, Kuala Lumpur, Malaysia.
Inspiration: Joel drew inspiration from multiple muses to create the Bee's Fizz cocktail. Firstly, the invention is a twist on a classic Bee's Knees, a prohibition era cocktail. Frequently made with honey, lemon and gin, Joel has based his formula on the recipe. And the second influence he comments, is his intention for the cocktail to be a "recreation of Gin & Tonic, the best gin cocktail/drink ever created."

BLYTHSWOOD SQUARE PUNCH

Glass: Collins
Garnish: Rosemary sprig & candied ginger
Method: SHAKE first 4 ingredients with ice and strain into ice-filled glass. TOP with cider.

45ml / 1½oz Caorunn Gin
15ml / ½oz Freshly squeezed lemon juice
15ml / ½oz Honey water 1:1
15ml / ½oz Fresh ginger juice syrup
5ml / ⅙oz Fernet Branca
45ml / 1½oz Medium dry cider
[Thistly Cross Traditional]

Origin: Created by Eduards Trofimcuks at Blythswood Square Hotel, Glasgow, Scotland.

Inspiration: Eduards' cocktail is named after Blythswood Square Hotel. "The place has a great history and is a great example of modern Scottish hotels," Eduards says. "Honey and ginger syrup is inspired by our own produce of honey, we actually have bees that make our own honey on the hotel's rooftop." And Eduards comments, most of the "ingredients are off the shelf, except ginger syrup which is super simple and fast to make... I've decided to use Fernet Branca, because it's one of our guests favorite digestifs after a good meal." A thoughtful recipe that has "a modern Scottish taste and character. Fresh with a spicy kick, complex and fruity."

BY THE SPEY

Glass: Collins
Garnish: Shiso leaf & lemon zest twist
Method: POUR all ingredients into ice-filled glass and briefly stir.

40ml / 1 ⅓oz Caorunn Gin
70ml / 2 ⅓oz Coconut water
2.5ml / ¹⁄₁₂oz Single malt scotch whisky
40ml / 1 ⅓oz Homemade apple-shiso-stevia Juice
20ml / 2/3oz Ginger beer

Origin: Created by Miguel Fernandez Fernandez at Octave, Bangkok, Thailand.
Inspiration: Miguel says, "The 'By the Spey' is inspired by Scottish traditions & progressive thinking."

"The flavor of apple is represented by Shiso combined with freshness of lemon and the acidity of tamarind. Ginger beer adds another layer of flavor, without losing the focus on Caorunn... clear as Scottish rivers."

CAPITOL APPLE G&T

Glass: Highball
Garnish: Green & red apple peel ribbons
Method: STIR first 4 ingredients with ice and strain into ice-filled glass. TOP with tonic.

45ml / 1½oz Caorunn Gin
20ml / ⅔oz Drambuie
30ml / 1oz Ginger-infused apple juice
7.5ml / ¼oz Freshly squeezed lemon juice
45ml / 1½oz Fever-Tree Tonic water

Origin: Created by Lamar Lusk at Charlie Palmer Steak, Washington, DC, USA
Inspiration: "The bottle of Caorunn reminded me of the US Capitol Dome, which we can see from our rooftop," Lamar says. Being inspired by landscapes can be an exciting and creative process, which as we see here, results in a sensational cocktail.

COMPOSITION NO.5

Glass: Wine glass
Garnish: Dill sprig, sliced apple & orange zest twist
Method: THROW first 4 ingredients with ice and strain into chilled glass. TOP with tonic water.

45ml / 1½oz Caorunn Gin
45ml / 1½oz Fresh apple juice (Granny Smith)
7.5ml / ¼oz Elderflower syrup
2 dashes Celery bitters
75ml / 2½oz Tonic water

Origin: Created by Supawit Muttarattana at Vesper, Silom, Bangkok, Thailand.
Inspiration: The Composition No.5 cocktail was inspired by the painting of the same name, created by Wassily Kandinsky. Supawit says, the intention here was to put "art into the drink." A fascinating idea to infuse art and cocktail making, resulting in a flavoursome blend.

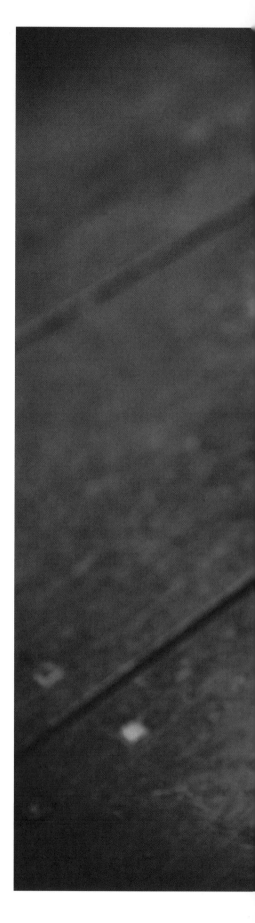

COUL BLUSH KELPIE

Glass: Old-fashioned
Garnish: Cross made from apple slices
Method: SHAKE first 4 ingredients with ice and strain into ice-filled glass. TOP with dandelion & burdock soda.

50ml / 1 ⅔oz Caorunn Gin
15ml / ½oz Freshly squeezed lemon juice
20ml / ⅔oz Freshly pressed apple juice
10ml / ⅓oz Agave syrup
40ml / 1 ⅓oz Fentimans Dandelion & Burdock

Origin: Created by Calum Macgregor, Leeds, Yorkshire, England.
Inspiration: Calum says, the Coul Blush Kelpie cocktail is "best enjoyed on a Scottish summer's day." Or ideally, it should be enjoyed whilst sat by the mythical Kelpies in Falkirk, which inspired the name. Calum spent a great deal of his childhood in Scotland with his father, and also drank plenty of Dandelion & Burdock and Irn-Bru. Calum kept this in mind when creating this recipe. He has combined Caorunn with Dandelion & Burdock for a strong, simple and refreshing cocktail.

THE CRUMMBLE LAND

Glass: Collins
Garnish: Apple slices dusted with cinnamon & flamed
Method: POUR ingredients into ice-filled glass. TOP with tonic and briefly stir.

40ml / 1 ⅓oz Caorunn Gin
7.5ml / ¼oz Fireball cinnamon whisky
5ml / ⅙oz Honey water
3 dashes Peychaud's Bitters
80ml / 2 ⅔oz Fever-Tree Mediterranean tonic water

Origin: Created by Soso Cheng & Jackie Saranyoo Vorasutr at Just a Drink, Bangkok, Thailand.
Inspiration: Created as a twist on the traditional gin & tonic, The Crummble Land is infused with spice, from the cinnamon dusted garnish to the cinnamon whisky.

Soso was inspired by apple crumble, resulting in a crafted cocktail that is a perfect accompaniment to the fruity dessert.

DIRK SWIZZLER

Glass: Collins
Garnish: Mint sprigs
Method: POUR all ingredients into glass 2/3 filled with crushed ice and SWIZZLE. Top with more crushed ice and swizzle to finish.

37.5ml / 1¼oz Caorunn Gin
22.5ml / ¾oz Mead
22.5ml / ¾oz Aperol
22.5ml / ¾oz Freshly squeezed lemon juice
15ml / ½oz Honey water

Origin: Created by Robert Land at Kiva Lounge, San Marcos, Texas, USA.
Inspiration: From Scottish influence and personal inspiration, the forming of the Dirk Swizzler came from two things. As a child, Robert was passionate about Scottish weaponry. Dirk, an old Scottish term meaning knife, was once carried by Scottish Highland soldiers. Robert has paired the term with his new love of the swizzle cocktail variety.

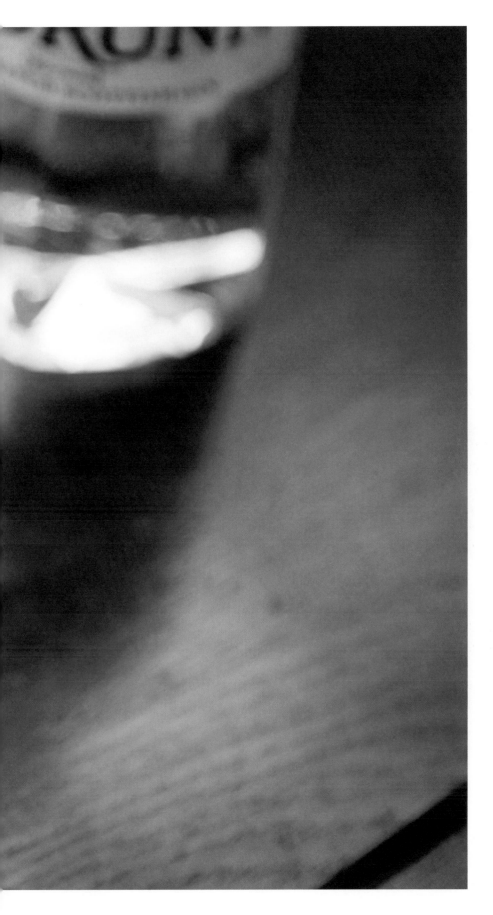

DOPO LA TEMPESTA

Glass: Old-fashioned
Garnish: Lime wheel & maraschino cherry
Method: MUDDLE sugar cube with gin until dissolved. Add other ingredients, STIR with ice and strain into ice-filled glass.

1 cube Sugar
50ml / 1 ⅔oz Caorunn Gin
2.5ml / ¹⁄₁₂oz Liquore al chinotto
15ml / ½oz Maraschino liqueur
2 dashes Peychaud's bitters

Origin: Created by Giorgio Pocorobba at American Bar, Rapallo, Italy.
Inspiration: Giorgio recounts when a very distinguished lady entered the American Bar. She asked that Giorgio crafted an original, fresh and full-bodied cocktail. He instantly thought of Caorunn Gin, knowing it worked perfectly as a base ingredient and was very versatile. Giorgio then invented an old-fashioned cocktail that revisited the roots of Caorunn's distillery in Scotland. With modern textures and notes, from the bitters and liqueur combination, he created a sumptuous cocktail: Dopo la Tempesta. And he notes, it was because he "started with excellent gin."

ESSENZIALE

Glass: Old-fashioned
Garnish: Edible flower
Method: SHAKE all ingredients with ice and fine strain into ice-filled glass (preferably over a chunk of block ice).

60ml / 2oz Caorunn Gin
5ml/ ⅙oz Fernet Branca
15ml / ½oz Italicus rosolio di bergamotto
5ml / ⅙oz Apple vinegar
1 spoon Pear jam

Origin: Created by Robert Pavel at The Fusion Bar & Restaurant, Florence, Italy.
Inspiration: "To create the mixture, I was inspired by the taste profile of Caorunn Gin and its botanicals, as well as its origin," Robert says. "To recreate the environment from where Caorunn is produced, I smoked the cocktail inside a bell with apple wood to remember the environment of whiskey and its peat… Finally, we decorate the cocktail with edible flowers to accentuate the floral notes of the product." The Italian inspired name, translated to essential, was chosen to highlight "a basic thing that you cannot live without" which Robert felt emphasised the choice of botanicals in Caorunn Gin. "Salute!"

FIVE INSPIRATIONS

Glass: Collins
Garnish: Red apple slices
Method: STIR all ingredients with ice and strain into ice-filled glass.

45ml / 1½oz Caorunn Gin
45ml / 1½oz Apple schnapps liqueur
10ml / ⅓oz Orange curacao
20ml / ⅔oz Apple juice
5ml / ⅙oz Lemon & lime juice
5ml / ⅙oz Sugar syrup

Origin: Created by Renato Salvatore at Lanificio San Salvatore, Salerno, Italy.
Inspiration: Renato says, "the inspiration comes from the simplicity of Caorunn Gin." The freshness of the apple and citrus notes of orange create an elegant and fruity cocktail. Renato created a blend which can be drunk on every occasion.

GHÀIDHEALTACHD

Glass: Old-fashioned
Garnish: Mint leaves, dehydrated apple
& elderflowers (when in season)
Method: SHAKE all ingredients with ice
and strain into ice-filled glass (preferably
over a chunk of block ice).

50ml / 1 ⅔oz Caorunn Gin
100ml / 3 ⅓oz Fresh green apple juice
5 fresh Mint leaves
30ml / 1oz Freshly squeezed lemon juice
15ml / ½oz Rose infused honey
(or floral honey)

Origin: Created by Francesco Serra at
Sketch Livorno, Italy.
Inspiration: Francesco says, the
inspiration came from "the Highlands, for
the name of the drink, the botanicals of
Caorunn Gin to keep flavour continuity
and the color of the drink reminds me of
the panorama of Scotland." The substitute
of honey for sugar is a delightful addition,
creating a sweet and floral cocktail.

GINGER MARY

Glass: Highball
Garnish: Mint sprigs & sliced chilli
Method: STIR all ingredients with ice and strain into chilled glass (no ice).

45ml / 1½oz Caorunn Gin
25ml / 5/6oz RinQuinQuin liqueur
40ml / 1 ⅓oz Carrot juice
20ml / ⅔oz Freshly squeezed lime juice
25ml / ⅚oz Honey infused with orange peel and chilli

Origin: Created by Michal Ubych at Chester IX, Aberdeen, Scotland.
Inspiration: Michal says, "my cocktail is inspired by one of the drinks from my childhood… multivitamin juice." And he comments, "for a long time I was looking for a decent replacement for the well known American Bloody Mary." Ginger Mary is the end delicious product of the two. The carrot creates the deep orange tones. "It's sweet, refreshing and thanks to chilli leaves a fantastic spicy aftertaste."

GOLDEN SPRITZ

Glass: White wine
Garnish: Lemon wheel & apple slice
Method: STIR first 4 ingredients with ice and strain into ice-filled glass. TOP with cava and briefly stir.

45ml / 1½oz Caorunn Gin
30ml / 1oz Fino sherry
30ml / 1oz Fresh pressed apple juice
22.5ml / ¾oz Homemade ginger syrup
60ml / 2oz Cava sparkling wine

Origin: Created by Jeff Carmichael at Capa at Four Seasons Resort Orlando, Orange, USA.
Inspiration: Fino sherry and cava, along with gin shine in this cocktail. Jeff works in a Spanish restaurant (Capa at Four Seasons) so he says, he "wanted to incorporate some Spanish elements as well as make a crisp refreshing summer cocktail."

HIGHLAND BLOSSOM

Glass: Rocks
Garnish: Lemon zest twist and Peychaud bitter float
Method: Fill glass with ice, add single malt scotch and set aside. Separately, STIR other ingredients with ice. Discard ice and scotch from glass and fill with fresh ice (preferably one large cube of block ice). Strain stirred ingredients into iced glass.

7.5ml / ¼oz Glenlivet 12-year-old Speyside single malt scotch whisky
45ml / 1½oz Caorunn Gin
15ml / ½oz Contratto Bitter liqueur (or Campari)
15ml / ½oz Rouge Gorge sweet vermouth
15ml / ½oz Meletti amaro

Origin: Created by Sean-Michael McCaffrey at Bishop & Bagg, Montreal, Canada.

Inspiration: Using Sean-Michael 's favourite alcohols, he created the Highland Blossom. He says, "The balance of bitter and sweet come from the two Italian products which round out the cocktail and remind me of a great Negroni combination I sell at Bishop & Bagg." And the forming of the cocktail's colouring was also an important part of the creation process, as Sean-Michael notes, "The Scotch rinse and peychaud bitter float are for aromatics and colour contrast which work with the yellow lemon zest." Sean-Michael believes a cocktail can be balanced with well portioned quality alcohol, which is why no extra sugar or syrups are added.

HIGHLAND SMASH

Glass: Old-fashioned
Garnish: Fresh sage & dehydrated apple slice
Method: MUDDLE sage in base of shaker. Add other ingredients, shake with ice and fine strain into ice-filled glass. Natalie's original recipe calls for 10 fresh micro sage leaves rather than the 2 regular sage leaves we've used.

2 fresh Sage leaves
50ml / 1 ⅔oz Caorunn Gin
30ml / 1oz Freshly squeezed lime juice
20ml / ⅔oz Fresh apple juice
15ml / ½oz Heather honey

Origin: Created by Natalie van Wyk at Dietrich's Luebeck An der, Luebeck, Germany.
Inspiration: This cocktail was inspired by "rugged mountains, colourful hills, and a sense of wilderness and mystery." Natalie says, it is because of the "spectacular landscapes of the Scottish Highlands," that she wanted to invent a cocktail which embodies the very place.

It is a twist on the modern classic Gin Basil Smash cocktail, using all-natural ingredients which Natalie found complemented Caorunn's botanicals.

HIGHLAND TONIC

Glass: Stemless snifter or red wine glass
Garnish: Edible flower
Method: SHAKE first 4 ingredients with ice and strain into ice-filled glass (preferably over a chunk of block ice). TOP with tonic.

60ml / 2oz Caorunn Gin
30ml / 1oz Fresh pressed apple juice
22ml / ¾oz Freshly squeezed lemon juice
15ml / ½oz Homemade sage syrup
60ml / 2oz Fever Tree Mediterranean Tonic

Origin: Created by Ryan Wolfe at Capa at Four Seasons Resort Orlando, Orange, USA.
Inspiration: "At my bar, we are lucky enough to have Caorunn on our menu in a classic style Spanish gin and tonic," Ryan says. "It has become the staple of our cocktail menu."

Ryan began with Caorunn Gin and crafted a recipe inspired by a gin and tonic. "I wanted to take that traditional cocktail and make a more progressive and modern style of drink. Caorunn's light and complex profile makes for a perfect base."

KEEP THE DOCTOR AWAY

Glass: Collins
Garnish: Dehydrated apple, heather flower, dry rose petals
Method: SHAKE first 5 ingredients with ice and strain into ice-filled glass. TOP with cider. (The original recipe calls for Quaglia Rosa rose liqueur.)

60ml / 2oz Caorunn Gin
15ml / ½oz Rose liqueur
22.5ml / ¾oz Freshly squeezed lemon juice
15ml / ½oz Raw Scottish heather honey
60ml / 2oz Apple cider

Origin: Created by Riccardo Rossi in Rome, Italy.
Inspiration: Riccardo says, inspiration came "from the botanicals of the gin. That's why the heather honey, the apple cider and the rose (rowan berry is from rose family)." Representing Caorunn Gin and its carefully handpicked Scottish botanicals, this cocktail is filled with wild ingredients transforming it into a well-balanced, delicious blend.

LOCH FIZZ

Glass: Highball
Garnish: Orange peel
Method: SHAKE all ingredients with ice and fine strain into chilled glass

50ml / 1 ⅔oz Caorunn Gin
10ml / ⅓oz AnCnoc peatheart
30ml / 1oz Freshly squeezed lime juice
40ml 1 ⅓oz Fresh apple Coul Blush juice
Top Mc Andrew Ale (Pale Ale)

Origin: Created by Patrick Piazza at Nat Cocktail House, Torino, Italy.
Inspiration: "Where can Gin and Scotch fall in love and get married?" Patrick asks. "In the Highlands."

Scottish flavours blossom in the cocktail, which Patrick says, is "an explosion of Scottish flavour." Topped off with a popular citrus scotch beer.

LOST & FOUND

Glass: Collins
Garnish: Li Hing Mui Plum Powder rimmed glass, garnished with apple slice & thyme sprig
Method: SHAKE first 4 ingredients with ice and strain into ice-filled glass. TOP with soda.

60ml / 2oz Caorunn Gin
30ml / 1oz Homemade apple & thyme shrub
15ml / ½oz Sugar syrup
6 dashes Angostura Aromatic Bitters
30ml / 1oz Soda water

Origin: Created by Buntanes Direkrittikul at Eat Me Restaurant, Bangkok, Thailand.
Inspiration: Beginning the research for a Caorunn cocktail, Buntanes says, "I was thinking how you can bring a sour and acidic flavour to the cocktail without using the citrus?" An interesting concept in itself. Buntanes comments, "The recent trend in the cocktail world is using different ingredients that are not typically in the bar inventory." Buntanes took to the kitchen shelves, and recounts "I am very lucky to have a kitchen full of fantastic ingredients available to me." A perfect place for a mixologist to find inspiration. Buntanes found an unusual item: a bottle of apple vinegar. "It made me think, that's such an interesting flavour and taste, also a very healthy ingredient, why not add it to the classic cocktail? This is how Lost & Found was born."

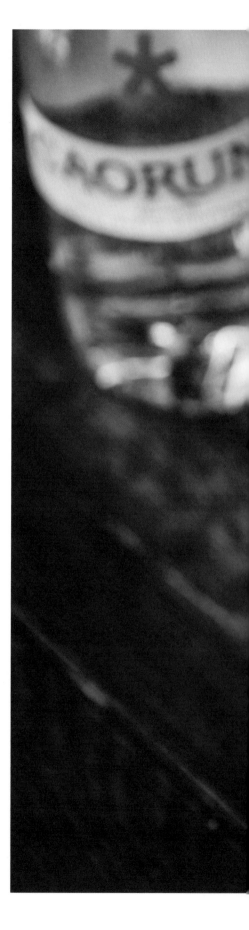

MIRAGE

Glass: Collins
Garnish: Dehydrated candied green apple slice
Method: SHAKE 4 ingredients with ice and strain back into shaker. DRY SHAKE (without ice) and fine strain into chilled glass (no ice). TOP with apple cream soda from a siphon.

60ml / 2oz Caorunn Gin
30ml / 1oz Freshly squeezed lime juice
15ml / ½oz Egg white
10ml / ⅓oz Sugar syrup (2:1)
Top with Homemade apple cream soda (from a siphon)

Origin: Created by Arvind Pillai at Screening Room Rooftop, Singapore.
Inspiration: From his time spent working on a rooftop bar, Arvind crafted the Mirage in response to Singapore's hot weather. By combining crisp flavours, he intended to create a refreshment to enjoy under the sun. Arvind says, the ingredients come together "not tarnishing the notes of the gin" but rather accentuating it, making a "fresh and elegant" cocktail.

ORCHARD BREEZE

Glass: Poco grande
Garnish: Honeycomb
Method: BLEND all ingredients with crushed ice and pour into glass.

60ml / 2 oz Caorunn Gin
22.5ml / ¾oz Freshly squeezed lime juice
22.5ml / ¾oz Velvet Falernum
120ml / 4oz Prosecco
1 scoop Homemade honey crisp apple sorbet (or other flavour of sorbet)

Origin: Created by Adrian Sarabia at The Downtowner, New Braunfels, Texas, USA.
Inspiration: The Orchard Breeze is a splendid take on the Italian Sgroppino Cocktail. Adrian comments "apple notes would pair well with the spices in the Falernum" for a bold and sweet taste. And after his recent experiments between sparkling wines and Gelato, Adrian has joined these ingredients for a uniquely flavoured cocktail.

PENTAGON

Glass: Collins
Garnish: Lemongrass straw
Method: SHAKE first 4 ingredients with ice and strain back into shaker. DRY SHAKE (without ice) and fine strain into chilled glass. TOP with soda.

50ml / 1 ⅔oz Caorunn Gin
10ml / ⅓oz Speyside single malt scotch whisky
30ml / 1oz Homemade lemon & honey mix
20ml / ⅔oz Egg white
25ml / ⅚oz Soda

Origin: Created by Anna Thomson at Tigerlily, Edinburgh, Scotland.
Inspiration: After Anna visited the Balmenach distillery (where Caorunn Gin is made), she was captivated. Anna says, she was mesmerised by the "spirit and community of the region, and the raw Scottish nature," and found herself inspired to create the Pentagon cocktail. And Speyside whisky has been included in the recipe to represent Scottish roots but also it accentuates the botanicals in Caorunn Gin. Anna notes, "This rework of the classic Silver Gin Fizz is a tribute to our 21st century Speyside culture."

THE PENTAGRAM SOUR

Glass: Rocks
Garnish: Lime wheel
Method: SHAKE all ingredients and strain into ice-filled glass.

45ml / 1½oz Caorunn Gin
15ml / ½oz St-Germain elderflower liqueur
15ml / ½oz Agave Nectar
20ml / ⅔oz Freshly squeezed lime juice
3 dashes Homemade green apple & dill tincture

Origin: Created by Lester Ligon at ABV, Makati City, Philippines.
Inspiration: "The number 5 has always been regarded as mystical and magical," Lester says on the choice behind the name, which connects to the 5 ingredients of this intriguing cocktail. Lester also notes the connection of 5 with Caorunn's 5 foraged Scottish botanicals, which has inspired the creation of The Pentagram Sour.
"The Pentagram Sour is truly a celebration of finding and bringing balance to everything we do in life… Every single ingredient has its own phenomenal character that brings its own distinctive personality into the drink which together creates a clever flavour combination."
Lester says, "Go ahead and let yourself enjoy a glass or two of the Pentagram Sour. Cheers!"

PENTAPPLE PUNCH

Glass: Collins
Garnish: Dehydrated apple slice
Method: SHAKE all ingredients with ice and strain into glass filled with crushed ice.

50ml / 1 ⅔oz Caorunn Gin
30ml / 1oz Sherry amontillado
60ml / 2oz Homemade pineapple shrub
30ml / 1oz Clear apple juice (not cloudy)
4 fresh Basil leaves

Origin: Created by Massimo Stronati at Vina Enoteca, Palo Alto, USA
Inspiration: Massimo's inspiration comes from one of the botanicals, the apple. "In Italy we have a lot of apple varieties and apples by the way are a versatile fruit and part of our Mediterranean diet," he says. "My father is having an apple after lunch and dinner for his entire life."

PINK EVERGREEN

Glass: Snifter
Garnish: Salt & brown sugar rim, garnish with rosemary sprig & pink grapefruit wedge
Method: SHAKE first 4 ingredients with ice and strain into glass filled with crushed ice. TOP with soda.

50ml / 1 ⅔oz Caorunn Gin
50ml / 1 ⅔oz Pink grapefruit juice
25ml / ⅚oz Homemade honey and rosemary syrup
2 dashes Angostura Aromatic Bitters
1 splash Soda water

Origin: Created by Lorenzo Varzi at Monboddo Bar, Edinburgh, Scotland.
Inspiration: Lorenzo says, "Rosemary and pink grapefruit have many health benefits for your body." Inspired to create a refreshing cocktail, Lorenzo says, the creation is an "easy-to-make cocktail… Making it with love, attention and the time it deserves, using homemade syrup, fresh rosemary and freshly squeezed pink grapefruit, the taste is real and refreshing."

RED BLOSSOM

Glass: Old-fashioned
Garnish: Dehydrated green apple slice, star anise & rosemary sprig
Method: SHAKE all ingredients with ice and fine strain into ice-filled glass (preferably over a chunk of block ice).

45ml / 1½oz Caorunn Gin
15ml / ½oz Raspberry puree
15ml / ½oz Homemade rosemary infused sugar syrup
20ml / ⅔oz Freshly squeezed lemon juice
70ml / 2 ⅓oz Cranberry juice

Origin: Created by Zainary Biju Til at P&C Cocktail Bar, Desa Sri Hartamas, Kuala Lumpur, Malaysia.
Inspiration: Inspired by different cuisines, Zainary's favourite dish of lamb accompanied by rosemary was the inspiration for the infusion of rosemary and sugar syrup. The Red Blossom cocktail combines traditional Malaysian elements, including star anise, an ingredient frequently found in Malaysian dishes.

THE ROYAL BALKAN

Glass: Highball
Garnish: Orange zest twist and mist with scotch whisky
Method: POUR ingredients into ice-filled glass and briefly stir.

45ml / 1½oz Caorunn Gin
30ml / 1oz Montenegro amaro
25ml / ⅚oz Bénédictine D.O.M. liqueur
2 dashes Grapefruit bitters
Top with Tonic water

Origin: Created by Jack Sleaford at Wood & Company, Manchester, England.
Inspiration: Jack was inspired to craft a cocktail that represented Irn-Bru. With recently changed ingredients, Jack intended The Royal Balkan to celebrate the soft drink's old, traditional recipe.

RUBY & DIAMOND

Glass: Old-fashioned
Garnish: Red apple slices & lemon zest twist
Method: STIR all ingredients with ice and strain into ice-filled glass (preferably over a chunk of block ice).

50ml / 1 ⅔oz Caorunn Gin
5ml / ⅙oz Green Chartreuse
5ml / ⅙oz Fino sherry
5ml / ⅙oz Homemade saffron syrup
5 dashes Peychaud's Bitters

Origin: Created by Vipop Jinaphan at Sugar Ray You've Just Been Poisoned, Bangkok, Thailand.
Inspiration: Named after its crystal clear and ruby colouring, the Ruby & Diamond was created to present the classical notes of old fashioned cocktails. The floral, herbal and spiced flavours merge seamlessly producing a refreshing and robust taste. Vipop comments, that the "beautiful note of saffron, chartreuse and peychaud" have been important in creating this distinct flavour.

RUNN CHAMBER NO.9

Glass: Collins
Garnish: Mint sprig, lemon peel and
Dandelion & Burdock Bitters
Method: SHAKE first 4 ingredients with
ice and strain into ice-filled glass. TOP
with tonic water.

60ml / 2oz Caorunn Gin
15ml / ½oz Suze Gentian liqueur
20ml / ⅔oz Homemade sage apple syrup
20ml / ⅔oz Freshly squeezed lemon juice
60m/ 2oz Tonic water

Origin: Created by M. Spencer Warren at
The Warren, Pittsburgh, Allegheny, USA.
Inspiration: "I was inspired by sitting in
a dandelion field in the middle of the
summer eating an apple in Scotland," M.
Spencer says. "What more would I want
than a refreshing Caorunn Gin cocktail to
gaze into the summer sky to pair with my
apple. It will cool me down and leave me
wanting another sip." It sure does leave us
yearning for more.

THE SCOT & THE TIGER

Glass: Old-fashioned
Garnish: Lychee & edible flower
Method: SHAKE all ingredients with ice and fine strain into ice-filled glass (preferably over block ice).

60ml / 2oz Caorunn Gin
30ml / 1oz Fresh apple juice
22.5ml / ¾oz Yuzu juice
30ml / 1oz Homemade lychee, lemongrass & sour plum infusion
15ml / ½oz Egg white

Origin: Created by David Koh at Bar Stories, Singapore.
Inspiration: David has been inspired by worldwide flavours, from the eastern tastes of yuzu and lychee, to the tastes of apple and sour plum. Creating a cocktail that encapsulates international flavours was the central focus of The Scot & The Tiger. David has infused Caorunn Gin with delightful fruits for a strong yet refreshing cocktail.

SCOTCH BONNET

Glass: Collins
Garnish: Dehydrated apple slice
Method: POUR all ingredients into ice-filled glass and briefly stir.

45ml / 1½oz Caorunn Gin
30ml / 1oz King's Ginger liqueur
20ml / ⅔oz Homemade spiced apple shrub
60ml / 2oz Soda water
2 dashes Angostura Aromatic Bitters

Origin: Created by Jessie Marrero at The Partisan, Washington, DC, USA.
Inspiration: "I wanted the apples and ginger to play off the gin. It's a smooth, yet subtly sweet and herbaceous drink," Jessie notes on the Scotch Bonnet cocktail. A balanced blend, the ginger notes give some added spice, making for a refreshing creation.

SCOTTISH APPLE SNAP

Glass: Collins
Garnish: Candied ginger, lemon wheel & apple slices
Method: SHAKE all ingredients with ice and fine strain into ice-filled glass.

60ml / 2oz Caorunn Gin
30ml / 1oz Freshly squeezed lemon juice
7.5ml / ¼oz King's Ginger liqueur
22.5m / ¾oz Homemade apple syrup (1:1)
3 dashes Apple bitters

Origin: Created by Ravinder Singh at Macellaio, Dallas, Texas.
Inspiration: Ravinder shares, "My friend makes an amazing wassail during the winter months that I thought would be lovely reimagined as a light and refreshing spring cocktail."
The ginger and apple complement each other, alongside the gin and lemon, which perfectly combine to form this snapping spring blend. Ravinder notes, "It's a cocktail that's made for the spring, yet reminds you of winter's past."

SCOTTISH RIFLE

Glass: Collins
Garnish: Dehydrated apple with anise candies (confetti)
Method: SHAKE all ingredients with ice and fine strain into chilled glass (without ice). TOP with chilled ale.

50ml / 1 ⅔oz Caorunn Gin
25ml / ⅚oz Drambuie
5ml / ⅙oz Branca Menta
15ml / ½oz Freshly squeezed lemon juice
60ml / 2oz Scotch ale beer

Origin: Created by Marco Carcatella at Amargo & Tasteit Viale, Reggio Emilia, Emilia Romagna, Italy.
Inspiration: "I wanted to express the Scottish spirit in this drink," Marco says. "I did a twist of French 75… Drambuie and beer with an Italian touch which exalt apple Coul Blush into Caorunn Gin with the balsamic of the mint."

SCOTTISH SUNRISE

Glass: Collins
Garnish: Float dashes of Angostura Bitters & garnish with spinach leaves
Method: MUDDLE spinach in base of shaker. Add next 3 ingredients, SHAKE with ice and fine strain into ice-filled glass. TOP with soda.

7 Spinach leaves
45 ml Caorunn Gin
15ml / ½oz Heather honey
30ml / 1oz Lemon juice
60ml / 2oz Soda water

Origin: Created by Mauro Uva at La Gineria, Padova, Italy.
Inspiration: Mauro was inspired to create a cocktail based upon the Scottish breakfast, those which are designed to give you energy for a long day. The crisp taste of the Scottish Sunrise cocktail is fresh and light.

SILENT BREEZE

Glass: Old-fashioned
Garnish: Mint sprig & dehydrated lemon
Method: SHAKE all ingredients with ice and fine strain into ice-filled glass.

50ml / 1 ⅔oz Caorunn Gin
25ml / ⅚oz Lychee liqueur
20ml / ⅔oz Homemade infused rose syrup
20ml / ⅔oz Freshly squeezed lemon juice
2 dashes Orange bitters

Origin: Created by Dailin Galea at Kingsway Valletta, Valletta, Malta.
Inspiration: Dailin recalls being inspired to create this cocktail when "sitting on the field eating lychee and smelt roses." The Silent Breeze cocktail combines lychee liqueur with fresh fruits which gives it sweet delectable notes.

SMOKEY SMOKE

Glass: Old-fashioned
Garnish: Dried tea leaves
Method: STIR marmalade with gin in base of shaker to help dissolve marmalade. Add other ingredients, SHAKE with ice and fine strain into ice-filled glass (preferably over a chunk of block ice).

2 tsp Orange marmalade
60ml / 2oz Caorunn Gin
30ml / 1oz Lapsang Souchong tea
20ml / ⅔oz Freshly squeezed lemon juice
10ml / ⅓oz Sugar syrup (2:1)

Origin: Created by Minh Duc Tran at Phatty 48, Vietnam.
Inspiration: The prominent and delicious smoky notes of the cocktail give it a distinctive essence. Lapsang Souchong tea is a smoky Chinese tea known for its antioxidants and health benefits.

SNAKE BERRY

Glass: Rocks
Garnish: Apple slice & blueberries
Method: SHAKE all ingredients with ice and fine strain into ice-filled glass.

50ml / 1 ⅔oz Caorunn Gin
20ml / ⅔oz Honey
¼ fresh Red apple (chopped)
10ml / ⅓oz Homemade blueberry & apple shrub
10ml / ⅓oz Freshly squeezed lemon juice

Origin: Created by Max Hanhike at Helsinki, Finland.
Inspiration: It was Caorunn Gin and its botanicals that inspired Max to craft the Snake Berry cocktail. "I got the inspiration to use blueberries in this cocktail after studying the Scottish Highlands," Max says. "I use fresh apple to deepen the apple flavors. Acidity comes from vinegar… Northern countries have used vinegar to preserve goods," Max notes after researching the use of these ingredients. "Honey is nature's own sweetener and here it fits perfectly to the flavor combination," Max says. "This is my image of the Scottish Highlands."

SNOW WHITE'S FIZZ

Glass: Collins
Garnish: Dehydrated apple slice & walnut sprinkle
Method: SHAKE first 4 ingredients with ice and strain into ice-filled glass. TOP with soda.

50ml / 1 ⅔oz Caorunn Gin
20ml / ⅔oz Cocchi Americano Rosa
30ml / 1oz Freshly squeezed lemon juice
30ml / 1oz Homemade red apple, cinnamon & roasted walnut shrub
Top with Soda

Origin: Created by Sudeera Fernando at Gold on 27, Burj Al Arab, Dubai, UAE.
Inspiration: Sudeera was inspired by red apples. Firstly, the red apple garnish complements 'the Caorunn Gin and tonic to highlight its aromatic flavour profile,' Sudeera says. But also, it is the red apple that is significant in the tale of Snow White, which has been inspiration for its name as well.

SPEYSIDE BLOSSOM

Glass: Highball
Garnish: Sliced apple fan & basil sprig
Method: MUDDLE apple and then basil in base of shaker. Add Caorunn Gin and cordial, SHAKE with ice and strain into glass filled with cracked ice. TOP with soda.

¼ fresh Red apple
4 fresh Basil leaves
60ml / 2oz Caorunn Gin
60ml / 2oz Homemade kaffir lime cordial
40ml / 1 1/3rd Soda

Origin: Created by Jaime Añon, Córdoba, Spain, 14008
Inspiration: Jaime was inspired by the valleys of Speyside. "The fresh herbaceous flavour of Caorunn," Jaime says was a significant aspect when crafting the cocktail. Jaime also paid attention to the balance of flavours, looking "to enhance the aroma and flavour of the gin."

SPLIFFICATED BEAT

Glass: Old-fashioned
Garnish: Lime zest twist
Method: SHAKE all ingredients with ice and fine strain into ice-filled glass. (Originally, this cocktail was served in a tonic bottle in a brown paper bag for the drinker to pour themselves.)

45ml / 1½oz Caorunn Gin
10ml / ⅓oz Orange curaçao
25ml / ⅚oz Beetroot syrup
25ml / ⅚oz Freshly squeezed lime juice
1 drop Black Walnut Bitters

Origin: Created by Pavel Zdarsky at The Spiffy Dapper, Singapore.
Inspiration: Pavel has combined the distinctive sweet and also savoury notes of beetroot with the zesty orange notes of curaçao. The beetroot also lends its vibrant colour to this attractive cocktail.

STONEWALL JACKSON

Glass: Old-fashioned
Garnish: Mint sprigs
Method: SHAKE all ingredients with ice and strain into ice-filled glass (preferably over a large cube of block ice). Note: Bryson's original recipe called for Uncouth Vermouth Apple Mint but as this is hard to obtain in Europe we substituted dry vermouth.

30ml / 1oz Caorunn Gin
30ml / 1oz Dry vermouth
30ml / 1oz St George spiced pear liqueur
15ml / ½oz Freshly squeezed lemon juice
7.5ml / ¼oz Cucumber syrup

Origin: Created by Bryson Ryan at FFC West Loop Health Club Cocktail Lounge, Chicago, USA.
Inspiration: The Stonewall Jackson Apple which can be found in Winchester, Virginia, inspired Bryson to invent the Stonewall Jackson cocktail. There's even an annual Apple Day Celebration at the Stonewall Jackson House. Showcasing this beloved fruit, Bryson has translated it here with the use of Vermouth Apple Mint, and a name that pays tribute to this treasured apple's homeland.

SUMMER BREEZE

Glass: Old-fashioned
Garnish: Pickled apple slice &
pomegranate seeds
Method: MUDDLE pickled apple and
pomegranate seeds in base of shaker. Add
other ingredients, SHAKE with ice and
fine strain into ice-filled glass.

⅛ whole Pickled red apple
2 spoons Pomegranate seeds
45ml / 1½oz Caorunn Gin
20ml / ⅔oz Freshly squeezed lemon juice
30ml / 1oz Heather honey

Origin: Created by Hans Roar Waaler at
Promenaden Bar & Brasserie, Risør,
Norway.
Inspiration: "When you look up at the
mountain in the Scottish Highlands on a
nice summer day, you will see the
mountains dressed up in the colourful
pink heather blossom," Hans says of what
inspired him to create the Summer Breeze
cocktail.

SWILCAN 700

Glass: Old-fashioned
Garnish: Lemon slice
Method: SHAKE all ingredients with ice and strain into ice-filled glass.

60ml / 2oz Caorunn Gin
22.5ml / ¾oz Sugar syrup (1:1)
7.5ml / ¼oz St-Germain elderflower liqueur
15ml / ½oz Campari
22.5ml / ¾oz Freshly squeezed lemon juice

Origin: Created by James Hayes at Rugan's, Burlington, Racine, USA.
Inspiration: Fruity, floral and herbal followed by dry lightly bitter finish, James says his cocktail is an "attempt to capture the taste of wild Scotland with a touch of refinement." It is named after the famous small stone Swilcan Bridge on the St Andrews Links golf course in Scotland. Originally to help shepherds to move their livestock, the bridge was built more than 700 years ago, and it is now customary for golfers to pay some homage to the bridge as they cross.

THYME & DANDY

Glass: Old-fashioned
Garnish: Dehydrated apple wheel
Method: SHAKE all ingredients with ice and strain back into shaker. DRY SHAKE (without ice) and fine strain into ice-filled glass.

60ml/ 2oz Caorunn Gin
20ml / ⅔oz Homemade apple & dandelion shrub
1 sprig Fresh thyme
15ml / ½oz Pedro Ximenez sherry
15ml / ½oz Egg white
2 dashes Orange bitters (optional)

Origin: Created by Kieran Collins, G1 Group Drinks Ambassador, Glasgow, Scotland.
Inspiration: "The inspiration for the Thyme & Dandy is to focus on two of the main botanicals used in Caorunn," Kieran says. "The dandelion greens & apple are combined in a shrub and shaken with thyme to create a balance of floral, sweet and bitter flavours." Kieran says, the egg white "provides a velvety texture which softens the sharpness of the shrub slightly."

THYME WILL TELL

Glass: Collins
Garnish: Caramelised apple slice &
thyme sprig
Method: SHAKE all ingredients with ice
and strain into ice-filled glass.

2 fresh Thyme springs
60ml / 2oz Caorunn Gin
50ml / 1 ⅔oz Fresh apple juice
30ml / 1oz Freshly squeezed lime juice
30ml / 1oz Homemade saffron syrup

Origin: Created by Karn Liangsrisuk at
RARB, Khet Phra Nakhon., Bangkok,
Thailand.
Inspiration: Thyme Will Tell was titled
after its signature ingredient, the thyme
herb. The first time Karn tasted Caorunn
Gin, he says 'the smell and the aromatic
from thyme' was prominent.
Karn has blended thyme with saffron
syrup and apple to produce a perfect sip
and savour cocktail.

VITAMIN B

Glass: Old-fashioned
Garnish: Orange zest twist
Method: SHAKE all ingredients with ice and fine strain into ice-filled glass.

60ml / 2oz Caorunn Gin
30ml / 1oz Lemon juice
15ml / ½oz Honey water
15ml / ½oz Apple juice
5ml / ⅙oz Fernet Branca

Origin: Created by Carlo "Billy" Schiattarella at Spaccio delle Carceri, Modena, Italy.
Inspiration: When Carlo spent a day behind the bar completely sick, he created this cocktail.
He says, "my mom always said to me 'an apple a day keeps the doctor away.'" And so, he took the traditional, family motto and used vitamin-packed ingredients. The Vitamin B cocktail has a vibrant, bright yellow colour.

YOU SHRUB UP WELL!

Glass: Wine glass
Garnish: Raspberry, apple slice & edible flower
Method: SHAKE first 4 ingredients with ice and strain back into shaker. DRY SHAKE (without ice) and fine strain into ice-filled glass. TOP with sparkling wine.

50ml / 1 ⅔oz Caorunn Gin
25ml / ⅚oz Freshly squeezed apple juice
20ml / ⅔oz Aqua faba (chick pea water)
30ml / 1oz Homemade raspberry & burnt wildflower honey shrub
25ml / ⅚oz Sparkling wine

Origin: Created by James Cooper at Shelley Yu's, Bangsar Baru, Kuala Lumpur, Malaysia.
Inspiration: At James' Scottish Grandma's house, fresh apple juice lay ready at breakfast, alongside wildflower honey and raspberry jam, which has been the inspiration behind the You Shrub Up Well cocktail. It represents James' Grandma in many ways. Even its name comes from the same phrase James' Grandma said when finding him dressed up: "Aye, don't you scrub up well!"

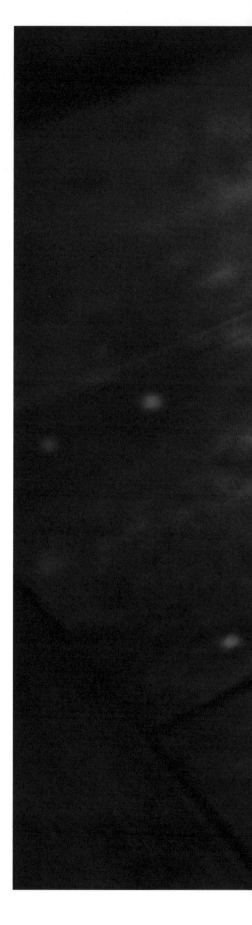

The Drinks

SHORT & STRAIGHT-UP DRINKS

ALCHEMIST'S ELIXIR

Glass: Coupe
Garnish: Apple cheveron on rim
Method: SHAKE all ingredients with ice and fine strain into chilled glass.

37.5ml / 1¼oz Caorunn Gin
10ml / ⅓oz Green Chartreuse
12.5ml / ⅖oz St-Germain elderflower liqueur
20ml / ⅔oz Freshly squeezed lemon juice
15ml / ½oz Egg white

Origin: Created by Matthew Ronald at Blue Dog, Glasgow, Scotland.
Inspiration: "The idea was to create something that little bit different and exciting whilst not detracting from the Caorunn itself," Matthew explains. "The unique botanicals of Caorunn allow it to carry its weight with modifiers that might mask other lesser distillates. The herbal notes just seemed a great match with the herbal essences of the Chartreuse and again with the floral notes of the St-Germain," Matthew says.

ANGELO'S SUMMER

Glass: Coupe
Garnish: Dehydrated red apple slice & lemon wheel crowned with edible flower
Method: SHAKE all ingredients with ice and fine strain into chilled glass.

45ml / 1½oz Caorunn Gin
15ml / ½oz Crème de violette [Briottet]
20ml / ⅔oz Freshly squeezed lemon juice
20ml / ²⁄₃oz Homemade orange & applewood smoked dulse syrup
15ml / ½oz Egg white

Origin: Created by Angelo Franchi at The White Horse, UK.
Inspiration: Angelo says he was inspired by "the arrival of sunny spring." The combination of springtime flavours shines through in Angelo's recipe. Angelo's Summer cocktail is light and vibrant which he intended would conjure images of spring when flowers begin to bloom, and a crisp chill lingers in the evening breeze.

APPLE BLUSH

Glass: Martini
Garnish: Rosemary sprig & red apple slice fan
Method: SHAKE all ingredients with ice and fine strain into chilled glass.

50ml / 1 ⅔oz Caorunn Gin
30ml / 1oz Apple juice (pink lady)
20ml / ⅔oz Freshly squeezed lemon juice
20ml / ⅔oz Homemade rosemary & cinnamon sugar syrup
3 drops Dashfire spiced apple bitters

Origin: Created by Enrico Calzuola at Experience Cafè, Rocca Imperiale, Italy.
Inspiration: "When Calabria meets Scotland," Enrico says of what inspired him to craft the Apple Blush cocktail. An essence of Scotland, firstly from Caorunn Gin, and also the apple notes that are prominent in the blend. But the Calabria flavours, rich and pleasant spices, stand out for a creative and flavoursome cocktail.

APPLE DAYS

Glass: Coupe
Garnish: Sugar crust rim, lemon zest twist (discard) & dehydrated apple slice
Method: SHAKE all ingredients with ice and strain back into shaker. DRY SHAKE (without ice) and fine strain into chilled glass.

50ml / 1 ⅔oz Caorunn Gin
20ml / ⅔oz Apple liqueur
25ml / ⅚oz Freshly squeezed lemon juice
10ml / ⅓oz Apple syrup
20ml / ⅔oz Egg white

Origin: Created by Cameron James Boyd at Hendricks Bar Four Seasons Jumeriah, Dubai, UAE.
Inspiration: "Apples Days takes inspiration from the saying 'The Apple doesn't fall far from the tree,'" James says of his Scottish heritage, a strong influence when inventing this recipe. James says, "my grandparents Scottish blood and how they influenced me to always remain positive through all situations in life," inspired him to craft a delightful and unique cocktail.

THE APPLE MAP

Glass: Coupe
Garnish: Dehydrated apple slice
Method: SHAKE all ingredients with ice and fine strain into chilled glass.

45ml / 1½oz Caorunn Gin
22.5ml / ¾oz Freshly squeezed lime juice
15ml / ½oz Homemade apple cider syrup
(2:1)
1 dash Old Pulteney 12-year-old Highland
single malt scotch whisky
2 dashes Teapot bitters

Origin: Created by Calvin Young at Cold Drinks Bar, San Francisco, USA.
Inspiration: "The inspiration for this cocktail really draws upon Caorunn Gin itself," Calvin explains. "After tasting Caorunn I noticed it resembled a London Dry Gin but with a refreshing finish. After reading more about Caorunn and how it's made, I decided that apple would be a great addition to this cocktail." Calvin created an apple cider syrup to complement the Caorunn Gin and to "add another layer of depth and complexity" to the cocktail. Calvin notes, "The name of this cocktail 'The Apple Map' draws its inspiration from the real 'Apple Map' that the Highland Council created. Since Caorunn uses the Coul Blush apple in its recipe, I thought it only fitting to pay homage."

AULD ALLIANCE

Glass: Coupe
Garnish: Sliced apple fan
Method: STIR Caorunn and apple jam in base of shake to help dissolve jam (or dry shake all ingredients prior to adding ice). Add other ingredients, SHAKE with ice and fine strain into chilled glass.

50ml / 1 ⅔oz Caorunn Gin
10ml / ⅓oz Homemade Coul Blush apple jam
7.5ml / ¼oz Calvados
15ml / ½oz Freshly squeezed lemon juice
2 dashes Lemon bitters

Origin: Created by Vincenzo Palermo at APT, Rome, Italy.
Inspiration: Calvados and Caorunn Gin are infused together in the Auld Alliance cocktail, meaning old alliance, in reminder of the alliance between Scotland and France which began in the 13th century. "The inspiration for this drink was to accentuate one of the botanicals present in Caorunn Gin, the apple." And so, Vincenzo prepared a homemade apple jam and balanced the flavours with lemon juice.

THE BALANCING ACT

Glass: Coupe
Garnish: Grapefruit zest twist
Method: SHAKE all ingredients with ice and fine strain into chilled glass.

45ml / 1½oz Caorunn Gin
30ml / 1oz Lillet Blanc
45ml / 1½oz Homemade tarragon sugar syrup (1:1)
30ml / 1oz Freshly squeezed grapefruit juice
2 dashes Orange bitters

Origin: Created by Samantha Tinyszin at Max Downtown, Hartford, CT, USA.
Inspiration: Through The Balancing Act cocktail, Samantha took on the challenge to create a cocktail for those of her guests who "don't like gin." Samantha has created "a smooth, balanced cocktail" which includes both savoury and citrus flavours, but with some prominent sweet notes in the mix as well. This blend is sure to turn a few minds with a dislike for the spirit.

THE BALLAD OF THE DANDELION

Glass: Tasting glass
Garnish: Orange zest twist & atomiser spray of dandelion root infused Caorunn
Method: SHAKE all ingredients with ice and strain back into shaker. DRY SHAKE (without ice) and fine strain into chilled glass.

60ml / 2oz Caorunn Gin
12.5ml / ⅖oz Homemade dandelion root syrup (2:1)
12.5ml / ⅖oz Freshly squeezed orange juice
25ml / ⅚oz Egg white (pasteurised)
1 pinch Scottish rock salt

Origin: Created by Antony Pearman at Alston Bar & Beef, Manchester, England.
Inspiration: The delicate flavours of Caorunn Gin are brought out in Antony's cocktail. Antony says, "using freshly squeezed orange to replicate the orange peel and also making a dandelion root syrup to replicate the great edition of dandelion leaves." Caorunn Gin's unique blend of 11 botanicals are pleasantly accentuated here in the Scottish Gin Twist. Consequently, Antony used 11g of dandelion root in his apple syrup to symbolise the botanicals.

THE BALMENACH

Glass: Martini
Garnish: Drop Scottish summer harvest cold pressed rapeseed oil & coul blush apple fan garnish sprayed with Angostura Bitters mist.
Method: MUDDLE apple in base of shaker. Add other ingredients, SHAKE with ice and fine strain into chilled glass.

3 slices Apple
40ml / 1 ⅓oz Caorunn Gin
20ml / ⅔oz Freshly squeezed lemon juice
20ml / ⅔oz Honey syrup (2:1)
5ml / ⅙oz Jägermeister liqueur

Origin: Created by Hugo Tang at The Lounge, Edinburgh, Scotland.
Inspiration: "Being Eurasian," Hugo says, and "having worked in several cocktail bars in Scotland and cooking many local dishes… the combination of oil and honey was a unique twist on local, Scottish ingredients." Hugo has adapted these unusual ingredients in The Balmenach for a unique and enjoyable cocktail.

BOUND BY HERBS

Glass: Coupe
Garnish: Lemon zest twist
Method: STIR all ingredients with ice and strain into chilled glass.

60ml / 2oz Caorunn Gin
15ml / ½oz Cointreau triple sec
15ml / ½oz Bigallet China China
1 dash Angostura Aromatic Bitters
1 dash Bar Keep Apple bitters

Origin: Created by Griffin Keys at Boulevardier, Dallas, Texas, USA.
Inspiration: Griffin found inspiration from a Manhattan recipe for his Bound by Herbs cocktail, notably the colour, the garnish and the use of Angostura in the concoction. Griffin used Bigallet "because I thought an amaro would play well with the botanicals in the gin." Moving through to fruity and citrus ingredients, Griffin says, "apple and orange flavors pair quite nicely" for a full-bodied flavoured cocktail.

BUCKY REVIVER

Glass: Goblet
Garnish: Mint leaf
Method: SHAKE all ingredients with ice and fine strain into chilled glass.

50ml / 1 ⅔oz Caorunn Gin
30ml / 1oz White port (extra dry)
30ml / 1oz Italicus di Bergamotto
30ml / 1oz Freshly squeezed lemon juice
15ml / ½oz Homemade sea buckthorn syrup

Origin: Created by Oskar Wereża at Eliksir, Gdańsk, Poland.

Inspiration: "The inspiration for the Bucky Reviver was the Scottish countryside," Oskar says. "People there tend to get up very early, they are modest and humble," he continues. And that was the essence Oskar wanted to capture in the Bucky Reviver recipe. Oskar says, "using bergamot and sea buckthorn (which mimics apples and passion fruits) to enhance complex Scottish ingredients in Caorunn Gin like rowan berries and apples." Then, the appearance is simple, "served in a humble and minimalistic way, garnished with a dried mint leaf. A perfect way to start your day."

CAORUNN CIDER FLIP

Glass: Vintage coupe
Garnish: Line of Angostura Bitters across surface. Use pick to manipulate into wave pattern. Lightly sprinkle cinnamon.
Method: SHAKE all ingredients with ice and strain back into shaker. DRY SHAKE (without ice) and strain into chilled glass.

50ml / 1 ⅔oz Caorunn Gin
25ml / ⅚oz Freshly squeezed lemon juice
30ml / 1oz Homemade Cider &
cinnamon syrup
1 fresh Egg white
1 fresh Egg yolk

Origin: Created by Lee McIlhone at The WestRoom, Edinburgh, Scotland.
Inspiration: "The inspiration was the apple and cinnamon muffin I had for my breakfast from the bakery across the street… It was still winter and as well as the flavour profile, I wanted to make something that was filling and slightly warming," Lee explains on his inspiration for the Caorunn Cider Flip cocktail.

COLORUNN

Glass: Coupe
Garnish: Orange zest twist & lavender
Method: SHAKE first 4 ingredients with the ice and fine strain into chilled glass. TOP with sparkling water and briefly stir.

45ml / 1½oz Caorunn Gin
10ml / ⅓oz Monin Spicy Mango syrup
10ml / ⅓oz Elderflower syrup
15ml / ½oz Freshly squeezed lime juice
40ml / 1 ⅓oz Sparkling water

Origin: Created by Agnieszka Cieślar at Restauracja Beatris, Wisła, Poland
Inspiration: Agnieszka was inspired to craft a cocktail that symbolised the Scottish Highlands, its mountains and valleys. The Colorunn concoction is easy to prepare and Agnieszka says, "the combination gives an unusual taste when we shake them. Just like the mountains, when the sun sets, they take on a thousand colours." The colourful garnish brightens the cocktail as a final flourish.

CORPSE REVIVER NO. BRU

Glass: Nick & Nora
Garnish: Lemon zest twist & absinthe mist
Method: SHAKE all ingredients with ice and fine strain into chilled glass.

45ml / 1½oz Caorunn Gin
20ml / ⅔oz Irn-Bru
15ml / ½oz Cocchi Americano
10ml / ⅓oz Freshly squeezed lemon juice
10ml / ⅓oz Honey water

Origin: Created by Alex Williams at Discount Suit Company, London, England.
Inspiration: After growing up in Surrey, Alex says, "I'm possibly the most English sounding Scot in the world," although Alex's roots lay in Moray Firth, Scotland. Alex recalls, "some of my fondest memories come from summer sojourns in Cullen, where my grandparents lived, running amok on the beach with my wee brother glugging Irn-Bru."

Alex says, the soft drink is "weird and wonderful," which inspired The Corpse Reviver No. Bru.

THE COUL ROSE

Glass: Coupe
Garnish: Dehydrated apple wheel
Method: SHAKE all ingredients with ice and strain back into shaker. DRY SHAKE (without ice) and fine strain into chilled glass.

60ml / 2oz Caorunn Gin
25ml / ⅚oz Homemade apple & rosemary shrub
5ml / ⅙oz Rose water
20ml / ⅔oz Freshly squeezed lemon juice
25ml / ⅚oz Egg white

Origin: Created by Joseph Miller at Malmaison, Newcastle, England.
Inspiration: A thoughtful creation, The Coul Rose cocktail "encapsulates Caorunn Gin's heritage but pays homage to its locally-foraged botanicals," Joseph says. Caorunn Gin has a rich history. The Balmenach Distillery traces back to 1824, making it one of the oldest distilleries in the Speyside region of Scotland.
"The name 'The Coul Rose' comes from the apple that is used as one of the 11 foraged botanicals; the Coul blush apple," Joseph says.

Joseph's cocktail is an enjoyable Scottish inspired beverage, which Joseph notes, "resembles the ever-growing bartending process in Scotland that thrives on innovation and ever-changing culture."

DASTARDLY

Glass: Coupe
Garnish: Scorched pandan leaf
Method: SHAKE all ingredients with ice
and fine strain into chilled glass.

45ml / 1½oz Caorunn Gin
10ml / 1/3oz Suze liqueur
15ml / ½oz Freshly squeezed lemon juice
10ml / 1/3oz Calamansi juice
30ml / 1oz Homemade pandan syrup

Origin: Created by Mark John Herrera at
Yes Please, Taguig, Philippines.
Inspiration: "I want to highlight the
flavour of Asia," Mark says on his
Dastardly cocktail. Calamansi and pandan
are two Asian ingredients he uses in this
blend. They are distinctive flavours that to
the new palate, is an intriguing and
surprisingly delicious mixture. Mark says,
by "using our own products or produce
we can help promote the place we come
from." An aspiration Mark has achieved
by presenting these interesting flavours
that has us celebrating those aromatic
tastes native to Asia.

EASY D.

Glass: Flute
Garnish: None
Method: SHAKE first 4 ingredients with ice and fine strain into chilled glass. TOP with sparkling solution.

45ml / 1½oz Caorunn Gin
5ml / ⅙oz Islay single malt scotch whisky
20ml / ⅔oz Dry Riesling wine
10ml / ⅓oz Orgeat (almond) syrup
30ml / 1oz 5% salted sparkling malic acid solution (dissolve 3 flakes of maldon salt and 2.5g of malic acid powder in 50ml / 1 ⅔oz of ice cold sparkling water)

Origin: Created by Phil Robins at Redmonds, Glasgow, Scotland.
Inspiration: "The idea was to create a drink with both great depth of flavour but also layers of texture," Phil explains. He comments, "Subtle sweetness, a hint of smoke for the savoury element/a small amount of effervescence, designed to be easy drinking but also intriguing to your palate." These crisp, delicious flavours have an interesting depth that is truly enjoyable.

EPSILON

Glass: Coupe
Garnish: Orange zest twist
Method: STIR all ingredients with ice and strain into chilled glass.

45ml / 1½oz Caorunn Gin
15ml / ½oz Pineapple liqueur
7.5ml / ¼oz Amontillado sherry
45ml / 1½oz Indian tonic water
1 dash Orange bitters

Origin: Created by Wareewan Yodkamol at Bunker, Bangkok, Thailand.
Inspiration: Wareewan has created a cocktail which is refreshing and crisp, saying the Epsilon is "not too complicated to understand." Wareewan was inspired to invent a recipe which was easy to drink and easy to make.

FIFTH GREAL

Glass: Coupe
Garnish: Dehydrated apple cut around the 5 seed places
Method: MUDDLE olives in base of shaker. Add other ingredients, SHAKE with ice and fine strain into chilled glass.

2 Green olives (pitted)
50ml / 1 ⅔oz Caorunn Gin
15ml / ½oz Bénédictine D.O.M.
20ml / ⅔oz Homemade soft apple citric acid
5ml / ⅙oz Sugar syrup (1:1)

Origin: Created by Richard Kormos at GoodSpirit Whisky & Cocktail Bar, Budapest, Hungary.

Inspiration: Richard has created a "classic-style cocktail with herbal notes." A unique blend of aromatic ingredients, and in particular the Benedictine, which Richard notes, "is in my opinion a little bit - undeservedly - forgotten liquor nowadays."
"For me, Caorunn is a classic gin with a twist of Celtic spices," he notes. Richard researched Celtic Mythology to give his cocktail a name with Scottish origins. "I really like history which is also important for Caorunn, I think," Richard says.
"Greal is the philter of omniscience, made by Ceridwen goddess. What could be better than a cocktail of omniscience?"

FIVE 'N APP

Glass: Coupe
Garnish: Dehydrated apple slice
Method: MUDDLE fennel seeds in base of shaker. Add other ingredients, SHAKE with ice and fine strain into chilled glass.

½ spoon Fennel seeds
45ml / 1½oz Caorunn Gin
25ml / ⅚oz Freshly squeezed lemon juice
20ml / ⅔oz Pomegranate syrup
2 drops Saline solution

Origin: Created by Mark Velasquez at Shu, Belfast, Northern Ireland.
Inspiration: Mark says, his inspiration "is none other than the unique and traditional ingredient of Caorunn Gin which is the Coul Blush apple." Mark comments, "I wanted to create a cocktail that will look and taste like freshly squeezed apple juice." He explored Caorunn Gin's "versatility using different ingredients such as Fennel seeds." Mark notes, "I came up with the cocktail's name, Five n' App, to give emphasis to the five ingredients and my newly created apple-flavoured cocktail."

FLAT WHITE

Glass: Coupe
Garnish: Edible flower
Method: SHAKE all ingredients with ice
and fine strain into chilled glass.

50ml / 1 ²⁄₃oz Caorunn Gin
10ml / ¹⁄₃oz Fino sherry
5 dashes Orange bitters
2.5ml / ¹⁄₁₂oz Simple syrup (1:1)
*5ml / ¹⁄₆oz Citric acid solution [1tsp citric acid
dissolved in 90ml water]*

Origin: Created by Attapon De-Silva at
Q&A Bar, Wattana, Bangkok, Thailand.
Inspiration: The White Lady cocktail, a
classic, sour drink, was used as inspiration
in this invention. Attapon explains this
cocktail can be modified to adjust for
those who are concerned of drinking egg
whites or for vegans.

FLYING ROWAN

Glass: Nick & Nora
Garnish: Apple leather roll &/or lemon zest twist
Method: SHAKE all ingredients with ice and fine strain into chilled glass.

45ml / 1½oz Caorunn Gin
10ml / ⅓oz Sauterne wine
15ml / ½oz Homemade Gastrique
10ml / ⅓oz Freshly squeezed lemon juice
15ml / ½oz Fresh red apple juice

Origin: Created by Ken Langenfeld at Monteiths, Edinburgh, Scotland.
Inspiration: Originally garnished with an apple leather roll, we replaced with a lemon zest twist to simplify but perhaps use simply as a garnish rather than expressing the peels oils over the drink. Ken says his cocktail was "inspired by the flying Rowan tree which is said to have strong properties against magic and sorcery." He also sought to pay tribute to the Rowan berries used as one of the botanicals in Caorunn gin.

FORAGER

Glass: Martini
Garnish: Birds eye chilli
Method: MUDDLE chilli in base of shaker. Add other ingredients, shake with ice and fine strain into chilled glass.

1 slice Birds Eye chilli (chopped)
45ml / 1½oz Caorunn Gin
30ml / 1oz Fresh apple juice
15ml / ½oz Homemade lemongrass syrup (1:1)
15ml / ½oz Freshly squeezed lime juice

Origin: Created by Jamie Rhind at The Bamboo Bar, Mandarin Oriental, Bangkok, Thailand.
Inspiration: Jamie recounts his memories of Scotland, saying "I have fond memories of visiting the Scottish Highlands, smelling the fresh cool air and feeling alive!" Jamie wanted to encapsulate those feelings in the Forager by creating a light and fresh taste. Currently living in Thailand, Jamie was also inspired to feature the country in this cocktail by incorporating lemongrass and chilli, two traditional Thai flavours.

THE FORAGER

Glass: Coupe
Garnish: Half of a fig
Method: SHAKE all ingredients with ice and strain back into shaker. DRY SHAKE (without) ice and fine strain into chilled glass.

45ml / 1½oz Caorunn Gin
10ml / ⅓oz Orchard pear liqueur
25ml / ⅚oz Freshly squeezed lemon juice
2 spoons Homemade fig & apple chutney
1 fresh Egg white

Origin: Created by Conor Jones at the Blythswood Square Hotel, Glasgow, Scotland.

Inspiration: Conor was inspired by his grandparents' garden. "All ingredients I used for my homemade chutney were found in my grandparents' garden, full of organic fruits and veg." Similar to Caorunn's gin master Simon Buley who personally forages for the Scottish botanicals infused in the spirit. But Conor explains, "my grandfather's garden, the Scottish outdoors and harsh weather," all inspired him to create The Forager cocktail.

FORBIDDEN FRUIT

Glass: Coupe
Garnish: Apple cube dusted with cinnamon on stick
Method: SHAKE all ingredients with ice and fine strain into chilled glass.

50ml / 1 ⅔oz Caorunn Gin
30ml / 1oz Apple juice
25ml / ⅚oz Freshly squeezed lemon juice
15ml / ½oz Cinnamon syrup
15ml / ½oz Egg white (pasteurised)

Origin: Created by Marco Zampilli at Sheket, Rome, Italy
Inspiration: The Forbidden Fruit cocktail is reminiscent of the apple pie Marco ate as a child. Marco recalls his memory, a sour apple flavour, which has been imitated in this cocktail, alike to a gin sour.

FORBIDDEN FRUITS

Glass: Coupe
Garnish: Float edible flower
Method: SHAKE first 4 ingredients with ice and fine strain into chilled glass. TOP with sparkling wine.

45ml / 1½oz Caorunn Gin
40ml / 1 ⅓oz Homemade apple shrub
1 spoon Bonne Maman Damson Plum Reserve
3 dashes Ferdinand's Sweet Symphony Reisling Quince Bitters
35ml / 1 ⅙oz English sparkling wine

Origin: Created by Jason Palmer at Mr Cooper's, The Midland Hotel, Manchester, England.
Inspiration: Apple, orchards and the Garden of Eden was the inspiration behind Jason's Forbidden Fruits cocktail. Jason says, "I wanted to showcase the Coul Blush apple botanical and bring it to the foreground through different ingredients." Jason notes "accentuating the gins affinity with the fruit" was the central focus of his cocktail.

HÈBEL

Glass: Coupe
Garnish: Blackberry &/or dehydrated lime slice
Method: MUDDLE blackberries in base of shaker. Add other ingredients, SHAKE with ice and fine strain into chilled glass.

4 fresh Blackberries
45ml / 1½oz Caorunn Gin
20ml / ⅔oz Tawny port
15ml / ½oz Vanilla sugar syrup
20ml / ⅔oz Egg white

Origin: Created by Vincenzo Lannino at Botteghe Colletti, Palermo, Italy.
Inspiration: Vincenzo was inspired by artist and photographer François Hèbel. The cocktail is textured, fruity and infused with vanilla notes. It's a full-bodied delight. If you're curious on what an art inspired cocktail might taste like, prepare yourself a Hèbel.

HERBS & SPICES

Glass: Coupe
Garnish: Cilantro/coriander leaf
Method: SHAKE all ingredients with ice and strain back into shaker. DRY SHAKE (without ice) and fine strain into chilled glass.

50ml / 1 ⅔oz Caorunn Gin
20ml / ⅔oz Freshly squeezed lemon juice
20ml / ⅔oz Homemade apple & Coriander cordial
5ml / ⅙oz Green Chartreuse liqueur
15ml / ½oz Egg white (pasteurised)

Origin: Created by Kyle Van Oosterum at The Adamson Restaurant and Bar, St Andrews, Fife, Scotland.
Inspiration: "I was inspired by the botanicals in Caorunn (primarily the apple and coriander)," Kyle says. He comments, he "wanted to create a fresh summery drink with just a touch of savoriness. Simple to drink and even simpler to make."

HIGHLAND MOOR

Glass: Rocks
Garnish: Rosemary sprig & apple slice
flambéed with brown sugar
Method: POUR green chartreuse into
glass over rosemary sprig, ignite and
allow to burn for 5 seconds before
covering glass to extinguish. SHAKE
other ingredients with ice and fine strain
into pre-prepared glass.

1 spoon Green Chartreuse
1 fresh Rosemary sprig
50ml / 1 ⅔oz Caorunn Gin
35ml / 1 ⅙oz Freshly squeezed lime juice
25ml / ⅚oz Homemade rosemary sugar syrup

Origin: Created by Sean Eden, Sweden.
Inspiration: The Highland Moor
encapsulates the fresh open countryside,
emphasised by the garnishing of a
rosemary sprig. The combination of
delicate flavours has complemented the
botanicals of Caorunn Gin, including this
distinct note of rosemary blending
impeccably with the heather, juniper and
angelica root notes of the gin.

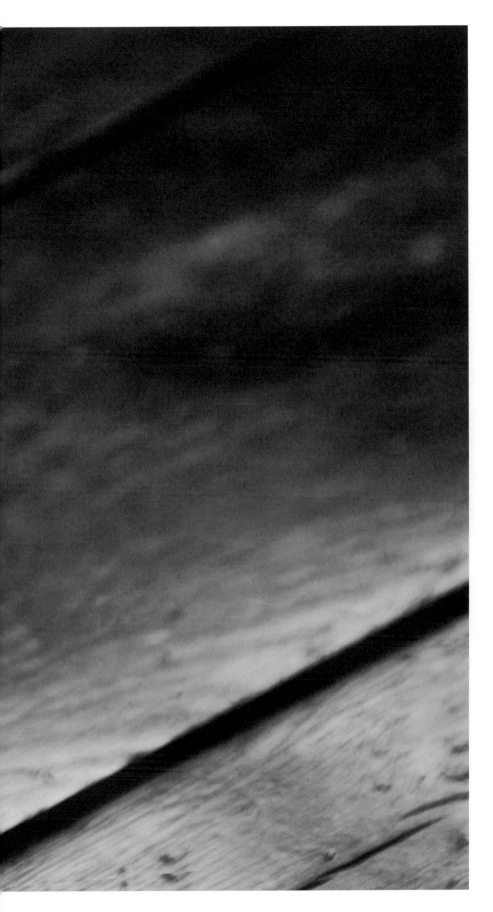

ICEBERG BLOSSOM

Glass: Coupe (preferably tall)
Garnish: Mint, thyme, edible flower, lemon zest & apple
Method: MUDDLE apple in base of shaker. Add other ingredients, SHAKE with ice and fine strain into chilled glass.

2 Apple wedges
50ml / 1 ⅔oz Caorunn Gin
50ml / 1 ⅔oz Aloe vera juice
1 sprig Mint (preferably water mint)
15ml / ½oz Homemade elderflower cordial

Origin: Created by Sebastian Kasyna at The Ivy City Garden, London, England.
Inspiration: A complex, all-year round cocktail. Speyside, home to over 50 distilleries, inspired Sebastian to create a concoction he says, is "cold but crisp in winter, refreshing in spring and naturally sweet in summer... Apple enhances Caorunn Gin, water mint gives fresh taste, elderflower gives sweetness and aloe vera combines all ingredients together."

ISABELLA'S RESTORATIVE DRAM

Glass: Nick & Nora
Garnish: Edible flowers
Method: All ingredients added to a shaker and given a steady dry shake. Ice added when foam is achieved. Cold shaken and strained into a Nick & Nora glass. (Optionally, lightly smoke cocktail with wood chips using a chef's smoker prior to shaking.)

45ml / 1½oz Caorunn Gin
22.5ml / ¾oz Cocchi Americano infused with Apple-Marjoram
7.5ml / ¼oz Maraschino liqueur
15ml / ½oz Freshly squeezed lemon juice
15ml / ½oz Egg white

Origin: Created by Sarah Anne Wollett at Luke's Kitchen & Bar, Maitland, Orange, USA.
Inspiration: "I had the great privilege of portraying Isabella Bird on stage in a production of Top Girls by Caryl Churchill," Sarah says. An Englishwoman by birth, Isabella Bird travelled abroad and detailed her adventures in A Curious Life for a Lady, which Sarah drew inspiration from. "Isabella Bird had a degenerative spinal disease but that never stopped her from being an intrepid explorer," Sarah notes. During Sarah's performance of Bird in Top Girls, she orders apple pie with cream. "It made sense to me to try to embody Isabella's choice of dessert in beverage form."

KING KA-ROON

Glass: Vintage goblet glass
Garnish: Dehydrated red apple slice
Method: SHAKE all ingredients with ice and strain back into shaker. DRY SHAKE (without ice) and fine strain into chilled glass.

45ml / 1½oz Caorunn Gin
50ml / 1 ⅔oz Fresh apple juice (preferably Coul Blush red apples)
40ml / 1 ⅓oz Homemade king ka mix
15ml / ½oz Maraschino luxardo
2 dashes Dandelion & Burdock Bitters

Origin: Created by Piero De Girolamo at Caffe Cavour, Rimini, Italy.
Inspiration: Piero was inspired by "the botanicals present inside the Caorunn Gin. The apple and the dandelion, as well as being two main ingredients of the gin, are two important ingredients of the drink." King Ka-Roon is a delicious blend, celebrating these foraged botanicals of Caorunn Gin.

LA REINE DES POMMES

Glass: Coupe
Garnish: Lemon zest twist (discarded)
Method: STIR all ingredients with ice and strain into chilled glass.

50ml / 1 ⅔oz Caorunn Gin
25ml / ⅚oz Christian Drouin Selection Calvados
5ml / ⅙oz Homemade honey water (2:1)
5ml / ⅙oz Bénédictine D.O.M. liqueur
2 dashes Orange bitters

Origin: Created by Pierre-Marie Bisson at Milk & Honey, London, England.
Inspiration: La Reine des Pommes translates as 'The Queen of Apples' a reference to both the use of Calvados apple brandy in this cocktail and Coul Blush apples also being one of the five Scottish botanicals in Caorunn Gin. This spirituous cocktail is both tasty and balanced.

LAST CANVAS

Glass: Old-fashioned
Garnish: Shot of dilute Islay single malt scotch whisky on the side
Method: SHAKE all ingredients with ice and fine strain into chilled glass.

45ml / 1½oz Caorunn Gin
5ml / ⅙oz Laphroaig Islay single malt scotch whisky
45ml / 1½oz Apple juice
40ml / 1 ⅓oz Homemade strawberry shrub made with apple vinegar and sugar
3 dashes Saline solution

Origin: Created by Mirko Turconi at Piano 35 Lounge Bar, Torino, Italy.
Inspiration: After seeing a painting of Scotland, Mirko created the Last Canvas as a tribute to the landscape. Both vivid and vast, Mirko felt the colours of Scotland, the earth, rock and undergrowth could be present in this cocktail. The Celtic roots, similar to the roots of Caorunn's very own wild botanicals, is at the centre of the Last Canvas. The apple tree which derives from Celtic culture, is present in both the gin and the ingredients Mirko uses.

LE FLEUR SAUVAGE

Glass: Coupe
Garnish: Lime zest twist
Method: SHAKE all ingredients with ice
and fine strain into chilled glass.

45ml / 1½oz Caorunn Gin
25ml / ⅚oz Elderflower liqueur
25ml / ⅚oz Freshly squeezed pink grapefruit
15ml / ½oz Honey syrup
1 dash Orange bitters

Origin: Created by Dylan Lewis Gosso at
Caffé della Posta, Bra, Piedmont, Italy.
Inspiration: Delving into the botanicals
of Caorunn Gin, Dylan's Le Fleur
Sauvage, meaning The Wild Flower,
combines Scottish botanicals, bitter fruits
and subtle honey notes for a distinctive
and original creation.

LIGHT KA-ROON SUMMER

Glass: Coupe
Garnish: Dehydrated apple slice
Method: THROW all ingredients with ice and strain into chilled glass.

45ml / 1½oz Caorunn Gin
15ml / ½oz Briotet Pamplemousse Rose
25ml / ⅚oz Apple juice
20ml / ⅔oz Freshly squeezed lemon juice
12.5ml / ⅖oz Sugar syrup

Origin: Created by Ite Kleefsman at Aberdeen, Scotland.
Inspiration: "The summery weather is asking for a fresh and light cocktail that one can enjoy during the day and later in the evening. Something crisp and clear like Caorunn itself," Ite says. And Caorunn Gin is indeed perfectly clear, which is effectively highlighted here in this cocktail with a blend that brings out those botanical notes of the gin.

MAKE ME BLUSH

Glass: Coupe
Garnish: Grapefruit zest twist
Method: STIR all ingredients with ice
and strain into chilled glass.

60ml / 2oz Caorunn Gin
30ml / 1oz Dry vermouth [Noilly Prat]
5ml / 1/6oz Luxardo Maraschino liqueur
5ml / 1/6oz Calvados
1 dash Orange bitters

Origin: Created by Joel Carleton at Bee's
Knees Bar Services, Winnipeg, Canada.
Inspiration: A balanced aromatic flavour,
the Make me Blush cocktail is inspired by
alcohol production in Scotland. The
country is home to a number of
distilleries, each with a rich history, often
making use of wild ingredients that can be
foraged. Earning its name from the Coul
Blush apples in the botanicals of
Caorunn, "a nod to the traditions of the
past," Joel says. The cocktail recipe is
based on the classic Martinez. That
includes the use of vermouth, gin as the
base spirit, and the delicate notes of
orange.

MELROSE GIN

Glass: Small wine
Garnish: None
Method: SHAKE all ingredients with ice and strain back into shaker. DRY SHAKE (without ice) and fine strain into chilled glass.

50ml / 1 ⅔oz Caorunn Gin
15ml / ½oz Calvados
20ml / ⅔oz Freshly squeezed lemon juice
37.5ml / 1¼oz Homemade rose and pomegranate syrup
15ml / ½oz Egg white

Origin: Created by Giuseppe Suriano at Da Giocondo, Rende, Cosenza, Italy. (Quantities divided by 1.2 from Giuseppe's original recipe.)
Inspiration: The MelRose Gin Cocktail combines the tastes of rose and pomegranate, for a striking flavourful combination. Giuseppe chose an interesting name, firstly to signify the ingredient of rose in the cocktail, but also, Melrose, the small town in Scotland.

MORNINGSIDE

Glass: Coupe
Garnish: Scorched dehydrated lime wheel
Method: SHAKE all ingredients with ice and fine strain into chilled glass.

35ml / 1 ⅙oz Caorunn Gin
15ml / ½oz 18.21 Apple Cardamom Shrub
15ml / ½oz Freshly squeezed lemon juice
15ml / ½oz Crème de cacao white
[Tempus fugit]
22.5ml / ¾oz Tempus Fugit Kina L'Aéro d'Or

Origin: Created by Shaun Stewart at The Elk Room, Baltimore, USA
Inspiration: Whilst trekking through the town of Morningside in Edinburgh, Shaun found the aroma in the air reminded him of Caorunn Gin. Possibly from the wild foraged Scottish botanicals that are infused in the gin, such as bog myrtle, dandelion leaf and heather.

ORIGINAL SIN

Glass: Coupe
Garnish: None
Method: SHAKE all ingredients with ice and fine strain into chilled glass.

60ml / 2oz Caorunn Gin
15ml / ½oz Calvilla AB Selezione apple liquor (or another high-quality apple liqueur)
15ml / ½oz Old Pulteney single malt scotch whisky
20ml / ⅔oz Freshly squeezed lime juice
10ml / ⅓oz Ginger syrup

Origin: Created by Andrea Jachetta at La Zanzara, Roma, Italy.
Inspiration: It was the "thought of the first original sin of Adam and Eve," Andrea says, that inspired the creation of the Original Sin cocktail. But also, Andrea notes, Scotland inspired this cocktail, from the use of scotch in the recipe and the flavour notes of apple. And it's the apple that is at the heart of the cocktail, both tempting and sweet.

OSMO CUP

Glass: Coupe
Garnish: Apple lollypop 4mm thick 2cm apple circle caramelised with sugar and torch and added popping sugar to one side & apple blossom (when available)
Method: SHAKE all ingredients with ice and fine strain into chilled glass.

50ml / 1 ⅔oz Caorunn Gin
7.5ml / ¼oz St-Germain elderflower liqueur
10ml / ⅓oz Chardonnay wine (non-oaked)
5ml / ⅙oz Giffard banane du bresil
15ml / ½oz Homemade osmose apple cordial shrub

Origin: Created by Patrick Vercambre at Pickardy Zeedijk, Belgium.
Inspiration: After competing in the Diageo Reserve World Class semi-final, showcasing an Irish whiskey and pear cocktail, Patrick has continued his experimentation with similar ingredients. Patrick says, "I decided to keep going in a similar direction because of the link between the gin and the apple." Patrick also explored the botanicals in Caorunn, finding elderberry and apple pairing with chardonnay, and rose, black tea and banana, created a harmonious balance. And the Osmo Cup has a sumptuous merging of tastes, each complementing one another.

PINK MOON

Glass: Martini
Garnish: Cucumber peel on stick
Method: SHAKE all ingredients with ice and strain back into shaker. DRY SHAKE (without ice) and fine strain into chilled glass.

50ml / 1 ⅔oz Caorunn Gin
25ml / ⅚oz Freshly squeezed lime juice
20ml / ⅔oz Monin Pomplemousse Rose (pink grapefruit) syrup
4 drops Lavender bitters (Scrappy's Bitters)
15ml / ½oz Egg white

Origin: Created by Marco Michelini at Must!, Roma, Italy.
Inspiration: Marco found inspiration in lavender to create the Pink Moon cocktail. "Lavender is anti-inflammatory, antiseptic and relaxing… the name of the cocktail derives precisely from the 'magic' use that was attributed to the lavender flowers," Marco explains. Lavender is "the flower of witches." It has "accompanied medieval recipes of northern Europe, has traveled from France to Scotland entering desserts and liqueurs." A very enchanting history, even the name represents the popular belief of the pink moon to signify rebirth during the spring solstice. "There is a famous recipe in Scotland… the lavender shortbreads… this cocktail is inspired by these lavender biscuits, changing the taste of orange with the slightly more bitter grapefruit."

THE PINK SLIP

Glass: Martini
Garnish: Float dehydrated lemon wheel
Method: SHAKE all ingredients with ice and fine strain into chilled glass.

60ml / 2oz Caorunn Gin
22.5ml / ¾oz St-Germain elderflower liqueur
15ml / ½oz Freshly squeezed lemon juice
15ml / ½oz Cranberry juice
22.5ml / ¾oz Lemonade

Origin: Created by Tyler Hill at Bar Liquorice, Baltimore, USA.
Inspiration: The Pink Slip brings forth the botanicals of Caorunn Gin. Tyler has created a harmonious balance between the fruity flavours. And The Pink Slip reminds us of Scotland's wild plants, both sweet and succulent.

THE PIPER'S KILT

Glass: Coupe
Garnish: Lemon zest twist & float of Islay single malt scotch whisky
Method: MUDDLE peppercorns and raspberries in base of shaker. Add other ingredients and stir to ensure honey is dissolved. SHAKE with ice and fine strain into chilled glass.

5 dried Pink peppercorns
5 fresh Raspberries
45ml / 1½oz Caorunn Gin
15ml / ½oz Freshly squeezed lemon juice
10ml / ⅓oz Honey

Origin: Created by Fique Zarate in Singapore.
Inspiration: "A twist on the classic Bee's Knees/Clover Club with fresh fruit and spice," Fique says. And The Piper's Kilt presents Scottish elements, from its name, to the blend, including "a touch a peat of Scottish Islay whisky," Fique notes, to create a unique cocktail.

PIQUANT C

Glass: Coupe
Garnish: Crust of dry powder of apple & cinnamon
Method: SHAKE all ingredients with ice and fine strain into chilled glass.

50ml / 1 ⅔oz Caorunn Gin
20ml / ⅔oz Freshly squeezed lime juice
15ml / ½oz Cinnamon syrup
15ml / ½oz Egg white (pasteurised)
1 dash Tabasco pepper sauce

Origin: Created by Marika Mazzesi at Cafè del Viale, Faenza, Italy.
Inspiration: "Apple, one of the main botanicals of Caorunn Gin," Marika says was the inspiration behind the Piquant C cocktail. "The Apple finds love when she meets cinnamon," resulting in a balanced and delectable blend. "The garnish enriches the sensory experience through view at first and smell,' Marika says. "I call my Sour Piquant C because it looks very feminine and the letter 'C' represents Cinnamon and Caorunn Gin."

REAL BEES KNEES

Glass: Coupe
Garnish: Dehydrated lemon slice
Method: SHAKE all ingredients with ice and fine strain into a chilled glass.

50ml / 1 ⅔oz Caorunn Gin
20ml / ⅔oz Freshly squeezed lemon juice
15ml / ½oz Homemade 3-Dimensional honey water
2 dashes Apple vinegar
1 dash Orange blossom water

Origin: Created by Dawid Pytkowski at El Koktel, Warsaw, Poland.
Inspiration: Dawid says, "As a young beekeeper and a serious nature lover I decided to create a drink with natural ingredients." The Real Bees Knees cocktail is a swish beverage which is a "twist on a classic Bees Knees," Dawid says. Honey is a signature ingredient here which gives the cocktail a finishing delightful taste. Dawid says, the cocktail is "a real spring spirit, a Real Bees Knees."

THE REMEDY

Glass: Martini
Garnish: Lemon 'flower' on stick
Method: STIR all ingredients with ice and strain into chilled glass.

50ml / 1 ⅔oz Caorunn Gin
20ml / ⅔oz Velvet Falernum liqueur
5ml / ⅙oz Rose water
7.5ml / ¼oz Citric acid solution [1tsp citric acid dissolved in 90ml water]
2 dashes Orange bitters

Origin: Created by Anna Zacharewicz at Boisdale of Bishopsgate, London, England.
Inspiration: "Sláinte!" Anna says, which is Gaelic for cheers. The Remedy cocktail is "fruity, fragrant, refreshing and easy to drink, yet classy and elegant," Anna notes. "I wanted to create a cocktail that initially looks exactly like a classic gin martini, being completely clear, but surprises you instantly after the first sip."

RETURN TO EDEN

Glass: Cocktail glass
Garnish: Dill sprig & pinch of red, black
& white pepper
Method: MUDDLE dill in base of shaker.
Add other ingredients, SHAKE with ice
and fine strain into chilled glass.

5g Dill leaves pulled from the stem
45ml / 1½oz Caorunn Gin
20ml / ⅔oz Brickford's cloudy apple cordial (or
substitute with 10ml fresh apple juice and 10ml
sugar syrup).
15ml / ½oz Organic apple cider vinegar
(diluted)
1 pinch Sea salt

Origin: Created by Poom Khamheang at
Drinksmith, Tambon Haiya, Amphoe
Mueang, Chiangmai, Thailand.
Inspiration: Poom describes the Return
to Eden as a "revival cocktail." The tastes
of sweet and aromatic notes are a perfect
balance with the botanicals of Caorunn
Gin. Poom intended the cocktail to use
natural ingredients, such as the sea salt
and organic apple cider vinegar, but also
the peppercorn and dill garnish. This
cocktail is a delicious spicy and sweet
infusion.

RUNNING IN THE HIGHLANDS

Glass: Coupe
Garnish: Orange zest twist & blackberry
Method: MUDDLE blackberries in base of shaker. Add other ingredients, SHAKE with ice and fine strain into chilled glass.

4 fresh Blackberries
60ml / 2oz Caorunn Gin
30ml / 1oz Lemon sherbet
15ml / ½oz Lillet Rose (camomile infused)
4 dashes Orange bitters [Scrappy's Seville]

Origin: Created by Jamie Oakes at Cure Restaurant and Bar, Unionville, Hartford, USA.

Inspiration: Jamie says, inspiration came from "my love of Scottish gin." The Running in the Highlands cocktail has both citrus and sweet flavours. "I have always loved creating cocktails with gin but, Scottish gins produce a better final product," Jamie says.

SANTO

Glass: Coupe
Garnish: Red apple slice
Method: SHAKE all ingredients with ice and fine strain into chilled glass.

45ml / 1½oz Caorunn Gin
15ml / ½oz Sathenay elderflower liqueur
40ml / 1 ⅓oz Apple (preferably Cool Blush) and cucumber shrub
20ml / ⅔oz Fresh Lime Juice
4 drops Dashfire Spiced Apple bitter

Origin: Created by Tommaso Scamarcio at Hagakure - Fusion E Sushi Restaurant Bar, Bari, Italy

Inspiration: Tommaso says "the principal botanical of the Caorunn, the Coul Blush apple" is the basis of the Santo cocktail. Crisp and delicious, fresh notes are brought to the foreground from the use of cucumber and apple. But Tommaso also looked to balance the acidity of the fresh lime juice with elderflower liqueur. A complex cocktail, Tommaso chose a cube of ice to symbolise the pure waters of the Scottish lakes. And to finish, Santo, meaning "Saint" in English, was chosen by Tommaso to pay homage to the Patron Saint of Scotland, Saint Andrew.

SCOTS BREAKFAST MARTINI

Glass: Martini
Garnish: None
Method: ADD all ingredients to shaker and stir to ensure jam dissolved. SHAKE with ice and strain back into shaker. DRY SHAKE (without ice) and fine strain into chilled glass.

45ml / 1½oz Caorunn Gin
2 spoons Blackberry (mure) jam
15ml / ½oz Freshly squeezed lemon juice
15ml / ½oz Egg white
30ml / 1oz Scottish lager beer

Origin: Created by Alen Lovkovic at 1897 Cigar Bar & lounge, Kempinski at the Wave, Muscat, Oman.
Inspiration: Alen says, inspiration came from "common Scottish household ingredients like fresh eggs and fruit preserves (for which it seems every house has a secret recipe)." And the Breakfast Martini embraces an inventive and resourceful recipe, as Alen says, is a shared tradition in Scotland. Easily finding inspiration in a Scottish pantry, Alen has crafted a delectable blend which would be rather delicious, enjoyed anytime of day.

SCOTS LAW

Glass: Coupe
Garnish: Thyme sprig
Method: MUDDLE berries and thyme in base of shaker. Add other ingredients, SHAKE with ice and fine strain into chilled glass.

2 fresh Brambles/blackberries
3 wild Thyme sprigs (just the leaves)
50ml / 1 ⅔oz Caorunn Gin
10ml / ⅓oz Freshly squeezed lemon juice
15ml / ½oz Honey water (1:1) [Heather]

Origin: Created by Luca Monetti at 24 Royal Terrace, Edinburgh, Scotland.
Inspiration: When Luca moved to Scotland, he was inspired by the country's nature and its abundance of wild herbs, brambles and thyme which grew within 100 yards of his workplace. Scots Law captures these natural elements, ingredients which can be handpicked on Scottish land. Luca says, "the right to roam gives you the opportunity to go wherever you want and therefore gather ingredients." Subsequently becoming a forager, Luca embraced Scottish culture showcasing it here in the Scots Law cocktail.

SCOTTISH GIN TWIST

Glass: Coupe
Garnish: Dehydrated apple slice
Method: MUDDLE raspberries in base of shaker, add other ingredients, SHAKE with ice and fine strain into chilled glass.

6 fresh Scottish raspberries
50ml / 1 ⅔oz Caorunn Gin
37.5ml/ 1¼oz Homemade apple syrup
12.5ml / ⅖oz Freshly squeezed lemon juice
15ml / ½oz Egg white

Origin: Created by Todd Robertson at Forgans, St Andrews, Scotland.
Inspiration: "I always loved Scottish raspberries growing up" Todd recounts. He has merged the raspberries with apples to create a pleasantly flavoured cocktail. Alike to Caorunn Gin, which is infused with wild Scottish botanicals, this cocktail embraces ingredients which can be homegrown in Scotland.

SENZA PAROLE

Glass: Martini
Garnish: Lime zest twist
Method: STIR all ingredients with ice and strain into chilled glass.

70ml / 2 ⅓oz Caorunn Gin
20ml / ⅔oz Liquore strega
15ml / ½oz Orange curaçao liqueur
15ml / ½oz Freshly squeezed lime juice
10ml / ⅓oz Homemade parsley syrup (2:1)

Origin: Created by Jacopo Misiano at L'Alchimista, Pistoia, Italy.
Inspiration: "My heart and my dream," Jacopo says on the inspiration for the Senza Parole. The name translates to 'without words' and gives the impression of a concoction that will leave us speechless. Try it and see for yourself.

SEONAIDH

Glass: Coupe
Garnish: Lavender sprig pegged to rim
Method: SHAKE all ingredients with ice and fine strain into chilled glass.

50ml / 1 ⅔oz Caorunn Gin
20ml / ⅔oz Calvados
15ml / ½oz Crème de framboise
25ml / ⅚oz Freshly squeezed lemon juice
10ml / ⅓oz Lavender syrup

Origin: Created by Jamie Graeme Gilmour at Masons, Manchester, England.
Inspiration: Inspired by Scottish culture, Jamie aimed "to add some fruitier, floral notes to the crisp freshness of Caorunn Gin." The potent taste of lavender is the central essence of the concoction. The Seonaidh has a delightful depth of flavour. And even its name has complexity. Seonaidh (pronounced shon-ey), comes from a Hebridean water spirit in Scottish folklore, known to be offered alcohol to ensure fertile ground and a good harvest.

SNOW WHITE'S MARTINI

Glass: Coupe
Garnish: Lemon zest twist
Method: STIR all ingredients with ice
and strain into chilled glass.

55ml / 1 ⅘oz Caorunn Gin
25ml / ⅚oz Drambuie
5ml / ⅙oz Pernod
2 dashes Bitter Truth Lemon Bitters
1 slice Lemon peel

Origin: Created by Narongsak
Thammasathiti at Mayuree Thai Tavern,
Baltimore, Maryland, USA
Inspiration: Narongsak found inspiration
from "the apple that Snow White ate in
the fairytale." A rather enchanting drink.

SONA

Glass: Wine glass
Garnish: Roasted bay leaf & dehydrated
green apple slice
Method: MUDDLE coriander in base of
shaker. Add other ingredients, SHAKE
with ice and fine strain into chilled glass.

2 sprigs Coriander leaves
60ml / 2oz Caorunn Gin
40ml / 1 ⅓oz Homemade orange & cardamom
sugar (1:1)
20ml / ⅔oz Apple juice
30ml / 1oz Calamansi lime juice

Origin: Created by Pranill Saam at
Genting Club, 360 Bar Genting, Genting
Highlands Resort, Pahang, Malaysia.
Inspiration: Sona, meaning gold,
wisdom and happiness, gave Pranill the
inspiration to craft this cocktail. And after
being inspired by Pranill's family, the
Sona cocktail is dedicated to Pranill's
mother & May Way.

SPRING STORM

Glass: Coupe
Garnish: Apple slice fan
Method: SHAKE all ingredients with ice and fine strain into chilled glass.

60ml / 2oz Caorunn Gin
5ml / ⅙oz Islay single malt Scotch whisky
20ml / ⅔oz Oleo Saccarum orange
20ml / ⅔oz Freshly squeezed lemon juice
15ml / ½oz Blueberry tea

Origin: Created by Roberto Belmonte at Hide Speakeasy, Caserta, Italy.
Inspiration: Taking inspiration from the Scottish landscape, Spring Storm was created in response to the diverse scenery from looming mountains to coastal farmland and meadows. It is a place rich with magnificent surroundings. And the Spring Storm has a similar delectable blend, the citrus is complemented by the sweetness of apple and blueberry.

STRAND 72

Glass: Coupe
Garnish: Dehydrated apple
Method: SHAKE all ingredients with ice and strain back into shaker. DRY SHAKE (without ice) and fine strain into chilled glass.

50ml / 1 ⅔oz Caorunn Gin
20ml / ⅔oz Sourz Apple liqueur
10ml / ⅓oz Green Chartreuse
30ml / 1oz Freshly squeezed lime juice
10ml / ⅓oz Egg white (pasteurised)

Origin: Created by Rumen Kostadinov at The Black Sheep, Sliema, Malta.
Inspiration: "With Caorunn Gin they fall in love easy," Rumen says on using Caorunn Gin to create the Strand 72 cocktail. "My biggest inspiration is to show the regular G&T drinkers, that they can enjoy their favorite gin in a great and well-balanced cocktail as well."

SUMMER ORCHARD

Glass: Coupe
Garnish: Juniper berries
Method: MUDDLE apple in base of
shaker. Add other ingredients, SHAKE
with ice and fine stain into chilled glass.
TOP with sparkling wine.

4 slices Red apple
45ml / 1½oz Caorunn Gin
10ml / ⅓oz Red wine vinegar
10ml / ⅓oz Watermelon syrup
Top with Sparkling wine

Origin: Created by Saimai Nantarat at A
Bar Rooftop, Klongtoey Bangkok,
Bangkok, Thailand.
Inspiration: "Caorunn and summer,"
Saimai says was the inspiration behind
the Summer Orchard cocktail. "Flavors of
the ripe apple brings out the notes of
Caorunn Gin, with round fruitiness from
the melon syrup." Saimai says, the
cocktail is "similar to a refreshing summer
fruit salad."

THREE PETALS

Glass: Coupe
Garnish: Lemon zest twist
Method: STIR all ingredients with ice and strain into chilled glass.

45ml / 1½oz Caorunn Gin
30ml / 1oz Lillet Rose
30ml / 1oz Rothman & Winter Orchard Pear Liqueur
3 dashes Fee Brothers Rhubarb Bitters
1 dash Angostura Orange Bitters

Origin: Created by Jon Black at Meat & Potatoes, Pittsburgh, Allegheny, USA.
Inspiration: "The inspiration for this drink was the change in seasons to spring time," Jon says. "My favorite time of year is when I can see the cherry blossom trees starting to bloom outside of my house. I wanted to create a drink that imitated the beautiful light pink color of the trees"
"A harmonious mix of flavors reminiscent of springtime," Jon comments on the Three Petals cocktail.

THYME FOR NETTLES

Glass: Coupe
Garnish: Viola and fresh thyme sprig
Method: SHAKE all ingredients with ice and fine strain into chilled glass.

40ml / 1 ⅓oz Caorunn Gin
10ml / ⅓oz Farigoule thyme liqueur
10ml / ⅓oz Homemade nettle syrup
15ml / ½oz Freshly squeezed pink grapefruit juice
2 drops Angostura Aromatic Bitters

Origin: Created by Christopher Resant at Hotel du Vin, Newcastle, England.
Inspiration: Christopher felt the poem (below) illustrated "the fresh breeze in the mountains of the highlands, subtle scents of peat with the animals roaming free." He says, "thinking of this poem makes me visualize." The essence of which has been poured into the crafting of the Nettles cocktail. And with such an evocative inspiration, Christopher has translated these visuals into flavours that capture those very elements, 'a sort of peaceful nature.'

Nettles
He describes
There's deer upon the mountain,
There's sheep along the glen,
The forests hum with feather,
But where are now the men?
Here's but my mother's garden
Where soft the footsteps fall,
My folk are quite forgotten,
But the nettle's over all.
The Poetry of Neil Munro
(Edinburgh: William Blackwood, 1931)

TO SPEY, FOR EVERYTHING

Glass: Flute

Garnish: Edible flower

Method: Rinse chilled glass with Pedro Ximinez sherry and set aside. SHAKE other ingredients with ice and strain back into shaker. DRY SHAKE (without ice) and fine strain into rinsed glass.

10ml / ⅓oz Pedro Ximénez sherry
45ml / 1½oz Caorunn Gin
15ml / ½oz Aperol
30ml / 1oz Fresh pressed rowan berry and apple juice
1 fresh Egg white

Origin: Created by Ross Parker at Arcane, Manchester, England.

Inspiration: Ross says, the cocktail recipe "is an ode to the River Spey. Paying homage to Caorunn's roots in Speyside." Speyside whiskies can be aged in sherry casks which inspired Ross to include the ingredient of sherry. Ross wanted to embody the place, in more ways than one, including the cocktail's light salmon colour which imitates the River Spey salmon. Ross says, he also "hand-pressed apples and rowan berries and used the juice from them in the drink to reference the unique Scottish botanicals in Caorunn."

TOUCH MALUM

Glass: Coupe
Garnish: Float star cut from apple
Method: MUDDLE apple in base of
shaker. Add other ingredients, SHAKE
with ice and fine strain into chilled glass.

¼ Fresh red apple
50ml / 1 ⅔oz Caorunn Gin
10ml / ⅓oz Drambuie liqueur
20ml / ⅔oz Freshly squeezed lemon juice
10ml / ⅓oz Homemade saffron syrup

Origin: Created by Top Samran
Tharasaeng at Hyde & Seek bar at the
Athenee Hotel, Groove @ Central Wold,
Bangkok, Thailand.
Inspiration: Inspired by the Garden of
Eden, where perhaps apples lay at the
heart of The Fall, if we're to read the
Biblical tale so closely. Top Samran's
cocktail represents this forbidden fruit,
one which we're told not to taste, but
when faced with the Touch Malum,
temptation gets the better of us in
the end.

UBHAL 75

Glass: Flute
Garnish: Apple slice around inside of rim
Method: STIR first 4 ingredients with ice and strain into chilled glass. TOP with cider.

50ml / 1 ⅔oz Caorunn Gin
15ml / ½oz Homemade apple cordial
10ml / ⅓oz Suze
5ml / ⅙oz White crème de menthe liqueur
80ml / 2 ⅔oz Dry cider

Origin: Created by Tymon Straburzyński at Lot Kury, Wrocław, Poland.
Inspiration: Tymon says, apple is "the most popular fruit in my homeland, Poland." Tymon intended to craft a "very refreshing, well balanced twist on a popular French 75 cocktail." The Ubhal 75, meaning apple in Gaelic, and 75 to highlight a fizzy cocktail, Tymon has created a beverage that is fruity and rather invigorating.
"Combined with mint liqueur (very popular combination in Poland), Suze for the perfect balance and fizzy dry hard cider to create a bridge between Scotland and Poland (with France in the middle)," Tymon says on what the Ubhal 75 offers.

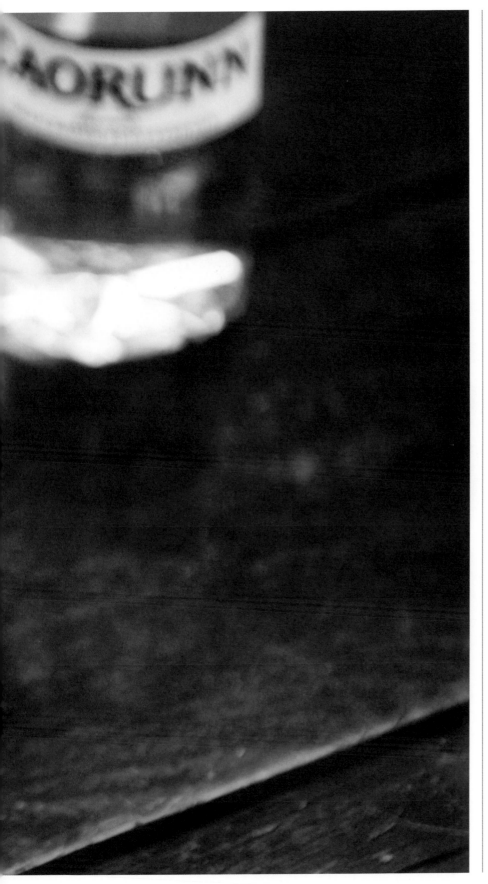

UBHAL OF MY EYE

Glass: Coupe
Garnish: None
Method: SHAKE all ingredients with ice
and fine strain into chilled glass.

45ml / 1½oz Caorunn Gin
30ml / 1oz Fresh apple juice
22ml / ¾oz Homemade honey syrup
(1:1 ratio)
15ml / ½oz Freshly squeezed lemon juice
1 dash Lavender bitters

Origin: Created by Ian Soukup at Verde
Kitchen & Cocktails, Bay Shore, New
York, USA.
Inspiration: This tasty gin and honey
sour has attractive lavender notes which
Ian says, "bring through a floral taste that
blends with Caorunn's botanicals." As for
the apple juice, "When I first tasted
Caorunn I knew that I wanted to make a
cocktail to showcase the apple flavor that
to me makes this gin stand out."
Incidentally, Ubhal is Scottish Gaelic for
apple.

URBAN SHERRY

Glass: Coupe
Garnish: Lemon zest twist
Method: STIR all ingredients with ice
and strain into chilled glass.

50ml / 1 ⅔oz Caorunn Gin
7.5ml / ¼oz Sacred English Amber Vermouth
7.5ml / ¼oz Tio Pepe fino sherry
5 drops Luxardo Maraschino liqueur
2 drops Lemon bitters

Origin: Created by Warakorn
Mathurunyanon at Teens Of Thailand,
Pom Prap Sattru Phai, Bangkok, Thailand.
Inspiration: "This spirit-forward cocktail
is made using simple ingredients,"
Warakorn says on his inspiration for
Urban Sherry. "This is a classy and elegant
drink, for the lovers of classic cocktails
that aren't afraid to experience
modern twists."
The ingredients Warakorn chose
"complement but amplify the wonderfully
unique characteristics of Caorunn Gin."

WHITE TALES

Glass: Coupe [costume coffee cup]
Garnish: Edible flowers
Method: SHAKE all ingredients with ice
and fine strain into chilled cup or glass.

45ml / 1½oz Caorunn Gin
15ml / ½oz Sauvignon Blanc wine infused with
oat meal overnight
15ml / ½oz Honey water (3:1)
20ml / ⅔oz Fresh apple juice
2 dashes Chocolate bitters

Origin: Created by Erzal Stiawan, The
Unlucky Cat Bar, Dubai, UAE.
Inspiration: Atholl Brose, a traditional
Scottish whisky beverage, inspired Erzal
to create the White Tales cocktail. Usually
it consists of oatmeal brose, honey, cream
and whisky. The concoction Erzal has
instead invented here is based upon those
same flavours but replacing the whisky
with Caorunn as the base spirit. This
twist on a classic cocktail is both
innovative and original reminding us that
fresh inventions are always great delights.

The Drinks

HOMEMADE INGREDIENTS APPENDIX

HOMEMADE INGREDIENTS APPENDIX

The following recipes have been collated from information provided by the bartenders who kindly contributed to this book, and from other sources. The publishers of this book disclaim any implied warranty for the suitability of these recipes and point out that the advice, methods and quantities expressed in these recipes may not be suitable for your situation.

APPLE & CORIANDER CORDIAL

By Kyle Van Oosterum, St Andrews, Fife, Scotland.
Take one apple (preferably Coul Blush, though Braeburn works just as well) and remove its core. Then take a handful of fresh coriander (roughly 40 grams) and dice finely. Throw both the diced apple and coriander into blender and purée until smooth then finely strain into a bowl. Measure the contents of the now-strained purée and add its equivalent in simple syrup (1:1).

APPLE & CUCUMBER SHRUB

By Tommaso Scamarcio, Bari, Italy.
Take 400g Cool Bush apple juice and 100g of cucumber juice and centrifuge to clarify. Mix juice with 2 small coffee cups of caster sugar for 24 hours in a bowl. Then add 2 small coffee cups of apple vinegar and mix. Filter, bottle and refrigerate.

APPLE & ROSEMARY SHRUB

By Joseph Miller, Newcastle, England.
Take: 2 apples chopped, 2 sprigs rosemary, 250ml sugar syrup, 250ml water and 250ml apple cider vinegar. Heat all ingredients in a pan until sugar dissolves. Leave on heat for 20 minutes and then strain into a sterilized container/bottle and refrigerate.

APPLE CIDER SYRUP

By Calvin Young at Cold Drinks Bar, San Francisco, USA.
Reduce a dry apple cider (I used "hatchet" from Sonoma, CA) on a stove by one-third. Remove cider from heat and add equal parts sugar and reduced cider (by weight). Be sure to blend it thoroughly. You can do so by using a whisk and mixing by hand. After the sugar is blended and completely dissolved into the cider, cover the solution and chill in the refrigerator for at least 12 hours.

APPLE CORDIAL

By Tymon Straburzyński at Lot Kury, Wrocław, Poland.
Dissolve 5g malic acid in 50ml apple syrup (e.g. Monin).

APPLE CREAM SODA

By Arvind Pillai, Singapore.
Combine the following in a siphon: 45ml egg white, 10 slices caramelised green and red apples (caramelise with butter and brown sugar), 350ml pressed apple juice and 9 drops vanilla bitters. Seal siphon and charge.

APPLE-SHISO-STEVIA JUICE

By Miguel Fernandez Fernandez at Octave, Bangkok, Thailand.
Infuse 10 Shiso leaves and 15 dried Stevia leaves in 1 litre clear apple juice over a low heat in a pan for 10 minutes. Allow to rest for 30 minutes and filter before use.

APPLE SHRUB

By Jason Palmer, Manchester, England.
Slice and blend 2 x Red apples (e.g. Coul Blush, Pink Lady or Royal Gala). Add 5 star anise and 125g Demerara sugar in a sterilised air tight container and leave for 12-24 hrs. Finally add 125ml Cider Vinegar, stir and filter through a muslin or Superbag. Bottle and keep refrigerated.

APPLE SYRUP (1:1)

Adapted from a recipe by Ravinder Singh at Macellaio, Dallas, Texas.
Dissolve 1 mug caster sugar into 1 mug freshly pressed apple juice in a pan over a low heat. Do not allow to boil. When sugar is fully dissolved, allow to cool, then strain, bottle and refrigerate.

APPLE SYRUP (2:1)

Adapted from a recipe by Todd Robertson, St Andrews, Scotland.
Dissolve 2 mugs caster sugar into 1 mug freshly pressed apple juice in a pan over a low heat. Do not allow to boil. When sugar is fully dissolved, allow to cool, then strain, bottle and refrigerate.

BLUEBERRY & APPLE SHRUB

By Max Hanhike, Helsinki, Finland.
200g frozen blueberries, 200ml apple vinegar, 50g fructose, boil in a pot, strain and bottle.

CIDER & CINNAMON SYRUP

By Lee McIlhone, Edinburgh, Scotland.
Heat equal parts sugar and cider in a saucepan with a pinch of cinnamon for every 100ml.

COUL BLUSH APPLE JAM

By Vincenzo Palermo, Rome, Italy.
Peel 1kg Coul Blush apples, divide them into quarters and remove the seeds, then cut them into slices and collect them in a bowl, sprinkling them with the juice of 2 lemons so that they do not darken. Collect them in a heavy-bottomed steel saucepan with 2 tablespoons of sugar (from total of 600g sugar). Stir well, put the saucepan on the stove and cook for 10 minutes from the time of boiling, stirring occasionally. At this point, pass the apples through a vegetable mill and pour the puree in the saucepan with the rest of the sugar and 1 stick of cinnamon. Cook for 25 minutes on low heat until the jam thickens. Pour while still hot into sterilised and pre-heated jam jars.

FIG & APPLE CHUTNEY

By Conor Jones, Glasgow, Scotland.
For a small batch you will need 2 green apples, 5 figs, 1 cinnamon stick, pressed apple juice and white caster sugar. Start by chopping the apples and figs into small cubes and adding them to a pot. Once in the pot cover with a cup of caster sugar and add to the heat to caramelise the apple and fig. Once caramelised add enough pressed apple juice to de glaze the pot (just enough apple juice to cover the content of the pot). Add cinnamon stick to the mixture and leave on heat to stew for 10 minutes. Once stewed add one more cup of sugar and crank up the heat till the liquid reduces. When little liquid remains take off the heat and let it cool. Add to jar and should last for up to 3 weeks if kept refrigerated.

GASTRIQUE

By Ken Langenfeld, Edinburgh, Scotland.
Caramelized sugar, deglazed with vinegar. Bring 300g of heather honey to the boil then simmer for 10 minutes, take off the heat and add 60ml of apple cider vinegar.

GINGER JUICE SYRUP

Adapted from a recipe by Eduards Trofimcuks at Blythswood Square Hotel, Glasgow, Scotland.
Combine ½ cup freshly extracted ginger juice with 1 cup of honey and stir well until the honey is fully dissolved. Allow to cool, bottle refrigerate.

GREEN APPLE & DILL TINCTURE

Adapted from a recipe by Lester Ligon, Makati City, Philippines.
Finely chop 7 sprigs of dill and 1 apple then place inside a clean jar. Pour vodka over and cover with a non-metal lid. Store in a cool and dry place and sit for up to 6-8 weeks. Check the tincture every week to ensure the apple and dill are fully submerged. Then filter, bottle and store in a cool, dry place.

HOMEMADE APPLE & THYME SHRUB

By Buntanes Direkrittikul, Bangkok, Thailand.
Infuse 1 litre apple cider vinegar with 2 green apples chopped into pieces and 50g thyme leaves. Sous vide for 60 minutes at 38°C. Then strain and refrigerate. If sous vide machine not available, it is possible to mix all ingredients together and keep in the fridge for 3 days. In this case the thyme leaves need to be muddled first.

HOMEMADE NETTLE SYRUP

By Christopher Resant, Newcastle, England.
Combine one bunch young nettles in a pot with boiling water and 500g caster sugar. Bring to boil and add the juice of 8 lemons and 4 cloves. When reduced, chill in a refrigerator for 2 hours and add more lemon peel to absorb the flavours.

HOMEMADE PANDAN SYRUP

By Mark John Herrera, Taguig, Philippines.

In a deep saucepan, place 1 cup granulated white sugar, 1 cup water and 4 pandan leaves and bring to the boil. Lower heat and simmer until sugar is dissolved. Remove pandan leaves, strain, bottle and refrigerate.

HOMEMADE PARSLEY SYRUP (SCIROPPO AL PREZZEMOLO)

By Jacopo Misiano, Pistoia, Italy.

Add 400g of parsley to a pan containing 500ml water and 800g of white sugar over a low heat. Stir until sugar fully dissolved. Allow to cool, then filter, bottle and refrigerate.

HOMEMADE ROSEMARY & GINGER SYRUP

Adapted from a recipe by Kiettisak Saleephan, Phuket, Thailand.

Dissolve 2 cups of sugar into one cup of water over low heat. Add 3 slices of ginger and 3 sprigs of rosemary, leave on heat (do not allow to boil) for five minutes. Allow to cool, strain, bottle and refrigerate.

HOMEMADE SOUR MIX

By Joel John Timis, Kuala Lumpur, Malaysia.

Combine 30ml freshly squeezed lemon juice, 30ml freshly squeezed lime juice, 30ml orange blossom water and 1 fresh egg white.

HONEY AND ROSEMARY SYRUP

By Lorenzo Varzi at Monboddo Bar, Edinburgh, Scotland.

Combine honey, water and rosemary in a small saucepan. Bring to the boil, stir occasionally. Remove the pan from the heat, let it sit and cool for 30 minutes before using.

HONEY CRISP APPLE SORBET

Adapted from recipe by Adrian Sarabia, New Braunfels, Texas, USA.

In a small saucepan, combine 2 diced apples and 4 tablespoons of lemon juice. Simmer on low heat (do not allow to boil) for five minutes or until apples are tender. Allow to cool. Stir in 2 tablespoons of honey then put the mixture in a blender with 2/3 cup of sugar and puree until smooth. Transfer the mixture to an ice cream machine and freeze according to manufacturer's directions. Leave the sorbet out to soften 10 minutes before serving.

INFUSED ROSE SYRUP

Adapted from a recipe by Dailin Galea, Valletta, Malta.

Infuse clean rose petals in 1:1 sugar syrup or substitute for a commercially available rose syrup diluted with equal parts water.

KAFFIR LIME CORDIAL

By Jaime Añon, Córdoba, Spain.

Made with water, sugar, lime juice and kaffir lime leaves, or substitute with equal parts lime cordial and water.

KING KA MIX

By Piero De Girolamo at Caffe Cavour, Rimini, Italy.

For 1 litre combine: 600ml fresh lemon juice, 400ml fresh orange juice, 25g egg white powder and 3 dashes orange flower water.

LEMON & HONEY MIX

By Anna Thomson at Tigerlily, Edinburgh, Scotland.

Combine 15ml lemon juice, 5ml honey and 10ml boiling water and stir until dissolved

LEMONGRASS SYRUP (1:1)

Adapted from recipe by Jamie Rhind, Bangkok, Thailand.

Dissolve 1 mugs caster sugar into 1 mug water in a pan over a low heat with a chopped lemongrass stem and simmer for 10 minutes. Do not allow to boil. When sugar is fully dissolved, allow to cool, then strain, bottle and refrigerate.

LYCHEE, LEMONGRASS & SOUR PLUM INFUSION

By David Koh, Singapore.

Empty 1 tin lychees with juice into a mixing jug. Add 10 chopped lemongrass stalks, and 10 seedless sour plums (Chinese dried preserved sour plums). Blend with immersion (hand) blender into fine puree. Leave mixture to sit in refrigerator overnight or at least 12 hours. Strain mixture though a chinois or fine strainer and bottle.

ORANGE & APPLEWOOD SMOKED DULSE SYRUP

By Angelo Franchi at The White Horse, UK.

Combine 5 grams Mara applewood and smoked Dulse seaweed, 1 peeled orange and 250ml sugar syrup (1:1) in a sauce pan over a low/medium heat for 15 minutes. Allow to cool, filter, bottle and refrigerate.

ORANGE & CARDAMOM SUGAR (1:1)

By Pranill Saam, Pahang, Malaysia.

Combine 500ml freshly squeezed orange juice, 500 grams granulated white sugar, 5 dried green cardamom pods (ratio one cardamom pod per 100 ml liquid) and blend until the sugar dissolves. Fine strain, bottle and refrigerate.

OSMOSE APPLE CORDIAL SHRUB

By Patrick Vercambre, Pickardy Zeedijk, Belgium.

Cut one apple very finely with a mandolin (do not shred otherwise you'll end up with a very milky syrup). Add same weight of sugar, a pinch of black tea and dried rose petals. Ideally, vacuum seal for 24hr or until the sugar dissolves or alternatively use a sealable glass jar. Strain into clean container and add same amount of apple cider vinegar and half of apple juice.

PINEAPPLE SHRUB

By Massimo Stronati, Palo Alto, USA.

Dissolve 300g sugar in 500cl freshly extracted and well filtered pineapple juice with sous vide at 55°C or in a saucepan over low heat. Add ascorbic acid and apple vinegar to taste and if you have the equipment to measure, then aim for a pH of 2.3. Be careful not to use too much vinegar and be sure sugar is fully dissolved.

RASPBERRY & BURNT WILDFLOWER HONEY SHRUB

By James Cooper, Kuala Lumpur, Malaysia.

Lightly muddle 250g raspberries and combine with 250ml apple cider vinegar in a kilner jar. Leave to infuse for 24 hours. Put 250g honey in a heavy bottom pan and heat until the honey boils (begins foaming). Reduce the temperature to a low simmer for 5 minutes. Pour the raspberry and honey mixture into the heated honey mixture, stir to combine and simmer for a further 2 minutes Fine strain to remove pulp, and chill before use.

RED APPLE, CINNAMON & ROASTED WAL-NUT SHRUB

By Sudeera Fernando, Dubai, UAE.

Combine 450g caster sugar, 150g red apple (sliced), 30g Oven Roasted crushed walnuts, 3g cinnamon in a sous vide bag, vacuum and leave at room temperature for 48 hours. Strain through a Superbag, bottle and refrigerate.

ROSE & POMEGRANATE SYRUP

Adapted from a recipe by Giuseppe Suriano, Rende, Cosenza, Italy

Combine 1 cup of fresh pomegranate juice and 1 cup of sugar over a low heat (do not allow to boil). And either add rose petals to the infusion or dashes of rose water. Allow to cool, strain, bottle and refrigerate.

ROSEMARY INFUSED SUGAR SYRUP (2:1)

Adapted from a recipe by Zainary Biju Til, Kuala Lumpur, Malaysia and Sean Eden, Sweden.

Dissolve 2 mugs caster sugar into 1 mug water in a pan with 3 rosemary sprigs over a low heat and simmer for 8 minutes. Do not allow to boil. When sugar is fully dissolved, allow to cool, then strain, bottle and refrigerate.

ROSEMARY & CINNAMON SUGAR SYRUP

Adapted from a recipe by Enrico Calzuola, Rocca Imperiale, Italy

Combine 1 mug of caster sugar with 1 mug of water over a low heat (do not allow to boil). Add 2 sprigs of rosemary and 1 cinnamon quill. Leave on heat for at least 5 minutes. Then allow to cool, filter, bottle and refrigerate.

SAFFRON SYRUP

Used in 3 recipes from Bangkok, Thailand.

Dissolve 200g caster sugar into 200g water in a pan with a pinch of saffron over a low heat and simmer for 8 minutes. Do not allow to boil. When sugar is fully dissolved, allow to cool, then strain, bottle and refrigerate.

SAGE APPLE SYRUP

Adapted from a recipe by M. Spencer Warren, Pittsburgh, Allegheny, USA.

In a saucepan over a low heat, combine 750ml apple juice, 20ml sugar and 2 sprigs of sage. Simmer on a low heat (do not allow to boil). Allow to cool, strain, bottle and refrigerate.

SAGE SYRUP

By Ryan Wolfe, Orange, USA

Steep 1/4 cup of torn sage leaves in 1 cup room temperature sugar syrup (2:1) for 1 hour and then strain.

SEA BUCKTHORN SYRUP

By Oskar Weręża, Gdańsk, Poland.

Mix 300g fresh sea buckthorn and 200g white sugar in a pan, put on low heat until the fruits start to crack, chill and strain.

SOFT APPLE CITRIC ACID

By Richard Kormos, Budapest, Hungary.

Combine 70ml apple juice, 30ml filtered water and 7g citric acid.

SPICED APPLE SHRUB

By Jessie Marrero, Washington, DC, USA.

This cold pressed shrub is made with 1 cup red apples, 1 cup caster sugar and 1 cup white wine vinegar. Leave apples and sugar to infuse with 2 cinnamon sticks, 1 star anise, and 2-3 cloves for roughly a day, covered in a refrigerator. Strain then mix with the vinegar and any leftover residual sugar.

STOUT REDUCTION

By Adam Day, Manchester, England.

Whisk the 100g golden caster sugar in 100ml Guinness stout in a pan on medium/high heat until it starts to boil. Reduce heat to a simmer and reduce the liquid by one-third. Allow to cool, bottle and refrigerate.

STRAWBERRY SHRUB

By Mirko Turconi, Torino, Italy.

Blend 150g wild strawberries with 100ml apple cider vinegar, 100ml water and 100g caster sugar. Filter, bottle and refrigerate.

TARRAGON SUGAR SYRUP (1:1)

By Samantha Tinyszin, Hartford, CT, USA.

Infuse 2 bunches of tarragon per quart/litre sugar syrup (1:1).

3-DIMENSIONAL HONEY WATER

By Dawid Pytkowski, Warsaw, Poland.

3-Dimensional honey water (AKA: Modern Classic Honey Water) is made by combining: 2 parts honey and 1 part preboiled water and 0.1 part propolis - bee glue alcohol extract.

COCKTAIL INDEX - BY COUNTRY

Belgium	Osmo Cup	Patrick Vercambre	129
Canada	Highland Blossom	Sean-Michael McCaffrey	55
Canada	Make me Blush	Joel Carleton	125
England	Adam's Apple	Adam Day	39
England	Angelo's Summer	Angelo Franchi	92
England	The Ballad Of The Dandelion	Antony Pearman	97
England	Corpse Reviver No. Bru	Alex Williams	104
England	Coul Blush Kelpie	Calum Macgregor	45
England	The Coul Rose	Joseph Miller	104
England	Forbidden Fruits	Jason Palmer	114
England	Iceberg Blossom	Sebastian Kasyna	119
England	La Reine des Pommes	Pierre-Marie Bisson	121
England	The Remedy	Anna Zacharewicz	135
England	The Royal Balkan	Jack Sleaford	68
England	Seonaidh	Jamie Graeme Gilmour	142
England	Thyme for Nettles	Christopher Resant	150
England	To Spey, For Everything	Ross Parker	152
Finland	Snake Berry	Max Hanhike	78
Germany	Highland Smash	Natalie van Wyk	56
Hungary	Fifth Greal	Richard Kormos	108
Italy	Apple Blush	Enrico Calzuola	94
Italy	Auld Alliance	Vincenzo Palermo	97
Italy	Dopo la Tempesta	Giorgio Pocorobba	49
Italy	Essenziale	Robert Pavel	51
Italy	Five Inspirations	Renato Salvatore	51
Italy	Forbidden Fruit	Marco Zampilli	114
Italy	Ghàidhealtachd	Francesco Serra	52
Italy	Hèbel	Vincenzo Lannino	114
Italy	Keep The Doctor Away	Riccardo Rossi	58
Italy	King Ka-roon	Piero De Girolamo	121
Italy	Last Canvas	Mirko Turconi	122
Italy	Le Fleur Sauvage	Dylan Lewis Gosso	123
Italy	Loch Fizz	Patrick Piazza	58
Italy	MelRose Gin	Giuseppe Suriano	126
Italy	Original Sin	Andrea Jachetta	128
Italy	Pink Moon	Marco Michelini	130
Italy	Piquant C	Marika Mazzesi	133
Italy	Santo	Tommaso Scamarcio	138
Italy	Scottish Rifle	Marco Carcatella	75
Italy	Scottish Sunrise	Mauro Uva	76
Italy	Senza Parole	Jacopo Misiano	142
Italy	Spring Storm	Roberto Belmonte	146
Italy	Vitamin B	Carlo "Billy" Schiattarella	88
Malaysia	Bee's Fizz	Joel John Timis	41
Malaysia	Red Blossom	Zainary Biju Til	67
Malaysia	Sona	Pranill Saam	144
Malaysia	You Shrub Up Well!	James Cooper	88
Malta	Silent Breeze	Dailin Galea	76
Malta	Strand 72	Rumen Kostadinov	148
Ntn Ireland	Five 'n App	Mark Velasquez	109
Norway	Summer Breeze	Hans Roar Waaler	82
Oman	Scots Breakfast Martini	Alen Lovkovic	139
Philippines	Dastardly	Mark John Herrera	105
Philippines	The Pentagram Sour	Lester Ligon	62
Poland	Bucky Reviver	Oskar Wereża	100
Poland	Colorunn	Agnieszka Cieślar	102
Poland	Real Bees Knees	Dawid Pytkowski	134
Poland	Ubhal 75	Tymon Straburzyński	154
Scotland	Alchemist's Elixir	Matthew Ronald	92
Scotland	The Balmenach	Hugo Tang	98
Scotland	Bee Simple	Alex Palumbo	40
Scotland	Blythswood Square Punch	Eduards Trofimcuks	41
Scotland	Caorunn Cider Flip	Lee McIlhone	101
Scotland	Easy D.	Phil Robins	106
Scotland	Flying Rowan	Ken Langenfeld	111
Scotland	The Forager	Conor Jones	113
Scotland	Ginger Mary	Michal Ubych	54
Scotland	Herbs & Spices	Kyle Van Oosterum	115
Scotland	Light Ka-roon Summer	Ite Kleefsman	124
Scotland	Pentagon	Anna Thomson	62
Scotland	Pink Evergreen	Lorenzo Varzi	65
Scotland	Scots Law	Luca Monetti	140
Scotland	Scottish Gin Twist	Todd Robertson	142
Scotland	Thyme & Dandy	Kieran Collins	84
Singapore	Mirage	Arvind Pillai	60
Singapore	The Scot & The Tiger	David Koh	73
Singapore	Splifficated Beat	Pavel Zdarsky	81
Spain	Apple & Caorunn	Jose Antonio Benitez Delgado	39
Spain	Speyside Blossom	Jaime Añon	79
Sweden	Highland Moor	Sean Eden	116
Thailand	Beauty & The Beast	Kiettisak Saleephan	39
Thailand	By The Spey	Miguel Fernandez Fernandez	42
Thailand	Composition No.5	Supawit Muttarattana	44
Thailand	The Crummble Land	Soso Cheng & Jackie Saranyoo Vorasutr	47
Thailand	Epsilon	Wareewan Yodkamol	107
Thailand	Flat White	Attapon De-Silva	110
Thailand	Forager	Jamie Rhind	112
Thailand	Lost & Found	Buntanes Direkrittikul	58
Thailand	Return to Eden	Poom Khamheang	137
Thailand	Ruby & Diamond	Vipop Jinaphan	71
Thailand	Summer Orchard	Saimai Nantarat	149
Thailand	Thyme Will Tell	Karn Liangsrisuk	87
Thailand	Touch Malum	Top Samran Tharasaeng	153
Thailand	Urban Sherry	Warakorn Mathurunyanon	156
UAE	Apple Days	Cameron James Boyd	94
UAE	Snow White's Fizz	Sudeera Fernando	78
UAE	White Tales	Erzal Stiawan	158
USA	The Apple Map	Calvin Young	96
USA	The Balancing Act	Samantha Tinyszin	97
USA	Bound by Herbs	Griffin Keys	100
USA	Capitol Apple G&T	Lamar Lusk	44
USA	Dirk Swizzler	Robert Land	47
USA	Golden Spritz	Jeff Carmichael	55
USA	Highland Tonic	Ryan Wolfe	56
USA	Isabella's Restorative Dram	Sarah Anne Wollett	121
USA	Morningside	Shaun Stewart	127
USA	Orchard Breeze	Adrian Sarabia	60
USA	Pentapple Punch	Massimo Stronati	63
USA	The Pink Slip	Tyler Hill	130
USA	The Piper's Kilt	Fique Zarate	131
USA	Runn Chamber No.9	M. Spencer Warren	72
USA	Running in the Highlands	Jamie Oakes	138
USA	Scotch Bonnet	Jessie Marrero	75
USA	Scottish Apple Snap	Ravinder Singh	75
USA	Snow White's Martini	Narongsak Thammasathiti	144
USA	Stonewall Jackson	Bryson Ryan	81
USA	Swilcan 700	James Hayes	83
USA	Three Petals	Jon Black	150
USA	Ubhal of my Eye	Ian Soukup	155
Vietnam	Smokey Smoke	Minh Duc Tran	76

COCKTAIL INDEX · BY BARTENDER

Bartender	Cocktail	Page
Adam Day	Adam's Apple	39
Adrian Sarabia	Orchard Breeze	60
Agnieszka Cieślar	Colorunn	102
Alen Lovkovic	Scots Breakfast Martini	139
Alex Palumbo	Bee Simple	40
Alex Williams	Corpse Reviver No. Bru	104
Andrea Jachetta	Original Sin	128
Angelo Franchi	Angelo's Summer	92
Anna Thomson	Pentagon	62
Anna Zacharewicz	The Remedy	135
Antony Pearman	The Ballad Of The Dandelion	97
Arvind Pillai	Mirage	60
Attapon De-Silva	Flat White	110
Bryson Ryan	Stonewall Jackson	81
Buntanes Direkrittikul	Lost & Found	58
Calum Macgregor	Coul Blush Kelpie	45
Calvin Young	The Apple Map	96
Cameron James Boyd	Apple Days	94
Carlo "Billy" Schiattarella	Vitamin B	88
Christopher Resant	Thyme for Nettles	150
Conor Jones	The Forager	113
Dailin Galea	Silent Breeze	76
David Koh	The Scot & The Tiger	73
Dawid Pytkowski	Real Bees Knees	134
Dylan Lewis Gosso	Le Fleur Sauvage	123
Eduards Trofimcuks	Blythswood Square Punch	41
Enrico Calzuola	Apple Blush	94
Erzal Stiawan	White Tales	158
Fique Zarate	The Piper's Kilt	131
Francesco Serra	Ghàidhealtachd	52
Giorgio Pocorobba	Dopo la Tempesta	49
Giuseppe Suriano	MelRose Gin	126
Griffin Keys	Bound by Herbs	100
Hans Roar Waaler	Summer Breeze	82
Hugo Tang	The Balmenach	98
Ian Soukup	Ubhal of my Eye	155
Ite Kleefsman	Light Ka-roon Summer	124
Jack Sleaford	The Royal Balkan	68
Jacopo Misiano	Senza Parole	142
Jaime Añon	Speyside Blossom	79
James Cooper	You Shrub Up Well!	88
James Hayes	Swilcan 700	83
Jamie Graeme Gilmour	Seonaidh	142
Jamie Oakes	Running in the Highlands	138
Jamie Rhind	Forager	112
Jason Palmer	Forbidden Fruits	114
Jeff Carmichael	Golden Spritz	55
Jessie Marrero	Scotch Bonnet	75
Joel Carleton	Make me Blush	125
Joel John Timis	Bee's Fizz	41
Jon Black	Three Petals	150
Jose Antonio Benitez Delgado	Apple & Caorunn	39
Joseph Miller	The Coul Rose	104
Karn Liangsrisuk	Thyme Will Tell	87
Ken Langenfeld	Flying Rowan	111
Kieran Collins	Thyme & Dandy	84
Kiettisak Saleephan	Beauty & the Beast	39
Kyle Van Oosterum	Herbs & Spices	115
Lamar Lusk	Capitol Apple G&T	44
Lee McIlhone	Caorunn Cider Flip	101
Lester Ligon	The Pentagram Sour	62
Lorenzo Varzi	Pink Evergreen	65
Luca Monetti	Scots Law	140
M. Spencer Warren	Runn Chamber No.9	72
Marco Carcatella	Scottish Rifle	75
Marco Michelini	Pink Moon	130
Marco Zampilli	Forbidden Fruit	114
Marika Mazzesi	Piquant C	133
Mark John Herrera	Dastardly	105
Mark Velasquez	Five 'n App	109
Massimo Stronati	Pentapple Punch	63
Matthew Ronald	Alchemist's Elixir	92
Mauro Uva	Scottish Sunrise	76
Max Hanhike	Snake Berry	78
Michal Ubych	Ginger Mary	54
Miguel Fernandez Fernandez	By The Spey	42
Minh Duc Tran	Smokey Smoke	76
Mirko Turconi	Last Canvas	122
Narongsak Thammasathiti	Snow White's Martini	144
Natalie van Wyk	Highland Smash	56
Oskar Wereża	Bucky Reviver	100
Patrick Piazza	Loch Fizz	58
Patrick Vercambre	Osmo Cup	129
Pavel Zdarsky	Splifficated Beat	81
Phil Robins	Easy D.	106
Piero De Girolamo	King Ka-roon	121
Pierre-Marie Bisson	La Reine des Pommes	121
Poom Khamheang	Return to Eden	137
Pranill Saam	Sona	144
Ravinder Singh	Scottish Apple Snap	75
Renato Salvatore	Five Inspirations	51
Riccardo Rossi	Keep The Doctor Away	58
Richard Kormos	Fifth Greal	108
Robert Land	Dirk Swizzler	47
Robert Pavel	Essenziale	51
Roberto Belmonte	Spring Storm	146
Ross Parker	To Spey, For Everything	152
Rumen Kostadinov	Strand 72	148
Ryan Wolfe	Highland Tonic	56
Saimai Nantarat	Summer Orchard	149
Samantha Tinyszin	The Balancing Act	97
Sarah Anne Wollett	Isabella's Restorative Dram	121
Sean Eden	Highland Moor	116
Sean-Michael McCaffrey	Highland Blossom	55
Sebastian Kasyna	Iceberg Blossom	119
Shaun Stewart	Morningside	127
Soso Cheng & Jackie Saranyoo Vorasutr	The Crummble Land	47
Sudeera Fernando	Snow White's Fizz	78
Supawit Muttarattana	Composition No.5	44
Todd Robertson	Scottish Gin Twist	142
Tommaso Scamarcio	Santo	138
Top Samran Tharasaeng	Touch Malum	153
Tyler Hill	The Pink Slip	130
Tymon Straburzyński	Ubhal 75	154
Vincenzo Lannino	Hèbel	114
Vincenzo Palermo	Auld Alliance	97
Vipop Jinaphan	Ruby & Diamond	71
Warakorn Mathurunyanon	Urban Sherry	156
Wareewan Yodkamol	Epsilon	107
Zainary Biju Til	Red Blossom	67

COCKTAIL INDEX - BY COCKTAIL NAME

Adam's Apple	Adam Day	39
Alchemist's Elixir	Matthew Ronald	92
Angelo's Summer	Angelo Franchi	92
Apple & Caorunn	Jose Antonio Benitez Delgado	39
Apple Blush	Enrico Calzuola	94
Apple Days	Cameron James Boyd	94
The Apple Map	Calvin Young	96
Auld Alliance	Vincenzo Palermo	97
The Balancing Act	Samantha Tinyszin	97
The Ballad Of The Dandelion	Antony Pearman	97
The Balmenach	Hugo Tang	98
Beauty & The Beast	Kiettisak Saleephan	39
Bee Simple	Alex Palumbo	40
Bee's Fizz	Joel John Timis	41
Blythswood Square Punch	Eduards Trofimcuks	41
Bound by Herbs	Griffin Keys	100
Bucky Reviver	Oskar Wereża	100
By The Spey	Miguel Fernandez Fernandez	42
Caorunn Cider Flip	Lee McIlhone	101
Capitol Apple G&T	Lamar Lusk	44
Colorunn	Agnieszka Cieślar	102
Composition No.5	Supawit Muttarattana	44
Corpse Reviver No. Bru	Alex Williams	104
Coul Blush Kelpie	Calum Macgregor	45
The Coul Rose	Joseph Miller	104
The Crummble Land	Soso Cheng & Jackie Saranyoo Vorasutr	47
Dastardly	Mark John Herrera	105
Dirk Swizzler	Robert Land	47
Dopo la Tempesta	Giorgio Pocorobba	49
Easy D.	Phil Robins	106
Epsilon	Wareewan Yodkamol	107
Essenziale	Robert Pavel	51
Fifth Greal	Richard Kormos	108
Five 'n App	Mark Velasquez	109
Five Inspirations	Renato Salvatore	51
Flat White	Attapon De-Silva	110
Flying Rowan	Ken Langenfeld	111
Forager	Jamie Rhind	112
The Forager	Conor Jones	113
Forbidden Fruit	Marco Zampilli	114
Forbidden Fruits	Jason Palmer	114
Ghàidhealtachd	Francesco Serra	52
Ginger Mary	Michal Ubych	54
Golden Spritz	Jeff Carmichael	55
Hèbel	Vincenzo Lannino	114
Herbs & Spices	Kyle Van Oosterum	115
Highland Blossom	Sean-Michael McCaffrey	55
Highland Moor	Sean Eden	116
Highland Smash	Natalie van Wyk	56
Highland Tonic	Ryan Wolfe	56
Iceberg Blossom	Sebastian Kasyna	119
Isabella's Restorative Dram	Sarah Anne Wollett	121
Keep The Doctor Away	Riccardo Rossi	58
King Ka-roon	Piero De Girolamo	121
La Reine des Pommes	Pierre-Marie Bisson	121
Last Canvas	Mirko Turconi	122
Le Fleur Sauvage	Dylan Lewis Gosso	123
Light Ka-roon Summer	Ite Kleefsman	124
Loch Fizz	Patrick Piazza	58
Lost & Found	Buntanes Direkrittikul	58
Make me Blush	Joel Carleton	125
MelRose Gin	Giuseppe Suriano	126
Mirage	Arvind Pillai	60
Morningside	Shaun Stewart	127
Orchard Breeze	Adrian Sarabia	60
Original Sin	Andrea Jachetta	128
Osmo Cup	Patrick Vercambre	129
Pentagon	Anna Thomson	62
The Pentagram Sour	Lester Ligon	62
Pentapple Punch	Massimo Stronati	63
Pink Evergreen	Lorenzo Varzi	65
Pink Moon	Marco Michelini	130
The Pink Slip	Tyler Hill	130
The Piper's Kilt	Fique Zarate	131
Piquant C	Marika Mazzesi	133
Real Bees Knees	Dawid Pytkowski	134
Red Blossom	Zainary Biju Til	67
The Remedy	Anna Zacharewicz	135
Return to Eden	Poom Khamheang	137
The Royal Balkan	Jack Sleaford	68
Ruby & Diamond	Vipop Jinaphan	71
Runn Chamber No.9	M. Spencer Warren	72
Running in the Highlands	Jamie Oakes	138
Santo	Tommaso Scamarcio	138
The Scot & The Tiger	David Koh	73
Scots Breakfast Martini	Alen Lovkovic	139
Scots Law	Luca Monetti	140
Scotch Bonnet	Jessie Marrero	75
Scottish Apple Snap	Ravinder Singh	75
Scottish Gin Twist	Todd Robertson	142
Scottish Rifle	Marco Carcatella	75
Scottish Sunrise	Mauro Uva	76
Senza Parole	Jacopo Misiano	142
Seonaidh	Jamie Graeme Gilmour	142
Silent Breeze	Dailin Galea	76
Smokey Smoke	Minh Duc Tran	76
Snake Berry	Max Hanhike	78
Snow White's Martini	Narongsak Thammasathiti	144
Snow White's Fizz	Sudeera Fernando	78
Sona	Pranill Saam	144
Speyside Blossom	Jaime Añon	79
Splifficated Beat	Pavel Zdarsky	81
Spring Storm	Roberto Belmonte	146
Stonewall Jackson	Bryson Ryan	81
Strand 72	Rumen Kostadinov	148
Summer Breeze	Hans Roar Waaler	82
Summer Orchard	Saimai Nantarat	149
Swilcan 700	James Hayes	83
Three Petals	Jon Black	150
Thyme & Dandy	Kieran Collins	84
Thyme for Nettles	Christopher Resant	150
Thyme Will Tell	Karn Liangsrisuk	87
To Spey, For Everything	Ross Parker	152
Touch Malum	Top Samran Tharasaeng	153
Ubhal 75	Tymon Straburzyński	154
Ubhal of my Eye	Ian Soukup	155
Urban Sherry	Warakorn Mathurunyanon	156
Vitamin B	Carlo "Billy" Schiattarella	89
White Tales	Erzal Stiawan	158
You Shrub Up Well!	James Cooper	88